LET'S TALK
ABOUT DEATH
OVER DINNER

LET'S TALK ABOUT DEATH (OVER DINNER)

AN INVITATION AND GUIDE TO LIFE'S MOST IMPORTANT CONVERSATION

Michael Hebb

Da Capo
LIFE
LONG

Da Capo Press
Hachette Book Group
1290 Avenue of the Americas, New York, NY 10104
www.dacapopress.com
@DaCapoPress

Printed in the United States of America
First Edition: October 2018
Published by Da Capo Press, an imprint of Perseus Books, LLC,
a subsidiary of Hachette Book Group, Inc.
The Da Capo Press name and logo is a trademark of The Hachette Book Group.

The Hachette Speakers Bureau provides a wide range of authors for speaking events. To find out more, go to www.hachettespeakersbureau.com or call (866) 376-6591.

The publisher is not responsible for websites (or their content) that are not owned by the publisher.

Editorial production by Christine Marra, *Marra*thon Production Services.
www.marrathoneditorial.org

Book design by Jane Raese
Set in 12.5-point Perpetua

Library of Congress Cataloging-in-Publication Data has been applied for.
ISBN 978-0-7382-3529-5 (hardcover); ISBN 978-0-7382-3531-8 (e-book)

LSC-C

10 9 8 7 6 5 4 3 2 1

Dedicated to my mom, Carole Hebb,
whose clear communication about
what she wants in life and death
formed the inspiration for this book.

In memory of Paul Hebb,
whose spirit lives in every dinner
and conversation about death
I have the honor to be a part of . . .

CONTENTS

CHAPTER 1. Offering Permission   1

CHAPTER 2. Extending the Invitation   17

The Prompts   35

*If you had only thirty days left to live, how would you
spend them? Your last day? Your last hour?*   **37**

*What foods do you remember a departed loved one cooking
for you?*   **49**

*If you were to design your own funeral or memorial,
what would it look like?*   **55**

Is there an excess of medical intervention at the end of life?   **62**

*Do you have your will, advance-care directives, and power of
attorney complete, and if not, why?*   **73**

*What is the most significant end-of-life experience of which
you've been a part?*   **80**

Why don't we talk about death?   **94**

How do you talk to kids about death?   **101**

Do you believe in an afterlife?   **108**

CONTENTS

Would you ever consider doctor-assisted suicide? **117**

*What song would you want played at your funeral?
Who would sing it?* **124**

Are you an organ donor? **131**

What does a good death look like? **139**

What do you want done with your body? **147**

Are there certain deaths we should never speak of? **159**

*If you could extend your life, how many years would you add?
Twenty, fifty, one hundred, forever?* **170**

What do you want your legacy to be? **179**

How long should we grieve? **188**

What would you eat for your last meal? **202**

Is there a way you want to feel on your deathbed? **206**

*What would you want people to say about you at
your funeral?* **211**

How do you end a conversation about death? **216**

Acknowledgments **223**

Recommendations for Further Reading **225**

Our Family of Resources **227**

Notes **232**

Index **239**

CHAPTER I

Offering Permission

The group of eight mostly strangers arrived on that blustery October night with a healthy amount of apprehension. Understandably so: they had accepted a dinner invitation to an evening titled "Let's Have Dinner and Talk About Death." My friend Jenna had dragged her husband, Brian, and her friend Molly, a physician, along. Then there was Cynthia, a student; Jasmine, a performance artist; Sandy, a documentary filmmaker; Joe, an entrepreneur; and Eleanor, new to Seattle and still grappling with the incessant darkness of her first northwest fall.

The door opened onto a loft with soaring twenty-five-foot ceilings, the corners piled high with books, Lego castles, a nest of crystals, and other strange artifacts. A king-size bed sat in the kitchen, and a piano, records, and a turntable filled out the room. If it weren't for the pleasant aromas bubbling out of a few simmering pots, the entire scene would have felt like a middle-aged hippie nightmare. Coats were thrown on the bed, and introductions crisscrossed the room. I kept cooking.

Much to my guests' surprise, I immediately gave them the task of setting the table, lighting the candles, and filling water glasses. We often make a great mistake when entertaining in the United States: we try to play God, or—worse yet—Martha

Stewart, and guests' only job is to be witty and appreciate the food. But humans are tribal creatures; we derive our value from what we contribute. So when people ask, as they unerringly do, "What can I do to help?" I always have an answer.

By the time we sat down, laughter had bubbled up more than a few times over the shared task of placing mismatched plates, silverware, and vintage wine glasses. The strangers were no longer covertly checking the time on their phones, wondering how long it would be until they were safely on their way home.

The room glowed amber. A dinner party should feel like a healthy secret. The lighting should remind us of childhood hours spent reading under our blankets with a dull flashlight. It is meant to evoke the campfire, the cave, the tree fort, the womb. Bright fluorescent lights are good for basketball games, but dinner parties wilt under these conditions.

The food was beautiful but simple: carrots blackened at the tips and swimming in fresh olive oil with Meyer lemon zest; savoy cabbage melted into sweetness with hard cider, thyme, and brown butter; black cod nudged against braised grapes and finished with Aleppo pepper and aged Banyuls vinegar. Each dish was arranged on a rustic platter, and the heavily aromatic air in the room let everyone know they had made the right decision coming to dinner.

There have been more than one hundred thousand of these dinners in the past five years, where strangers, friends, and coworkers gather around this seemingly awkward topic, and each dinner starts with the same simple offering. "Before we eat," I said, "I would love it if we could each honor someone who is no longer with us, someone who has died who had a positive impact on your life. I suggest you choose the first person who comes to mind. Don't edit here—they are first to your thoughts for a reason. Tell us their name and how they impacted your life, and then light a candle or raise a glass in their honor. And keep it to about a minute, as we all want to dig into this food."

It was quiet for only a moment before Cynthia, the youngest in the group, gave a spirited shout-out. "I want to raise my glass to Willibel Sutton, my grandmother. The toughest bitch who ever lived." Everyone laughed and clinked their glasses.

Cynthia then grew more earnest, carefully weighing her words. She told us how her grandfather, Bubba, wooed the difficult Willibel. He loved her more than anything in the world, constantly complimented her, and frequently said she'd look beautiful in a "toe sack" (potato sack). Night after night during their courtship he made her dinner. Each night, once she'd eaten, he'd silently rolled a single pearl across the table to her. She placed each pearl on a string around her neck so that, by the fortieth night, she had a full necklace. And that's when he proposed.

On its surface the story seems to be more about the romantic patience of Cynthia's grandfather than anything else. But as Cynthia reminded us, in the 1950s South it took a special sort of woman to command that level of devotion (and inspire a man to enter the kitchen in the first place, let alone for forty consecutive nights). Willibel defied all societal norms. Fiercely independent and highly intelligent, strong—and strong headed—she was a born leader. Her devotion to those lucky enough to know her was until death. As Cynthia spoke about missing her grandmother, she talked about the fiery advocate of equal rights and protections for the poor, but she also said, "I miss being loved by someone with the fierceness that Biddy loved me. She was my champion—singing my praises and cheering me on as I navigated through life, until she didn't have a voice."

Cynthia's toast demonstrates the intersection of grief, humor, joy, pain, loss, personal history, and the desire to connect deeply with other humans that emerges at these dinners. These components are at the heart of the topics of death, dying, and mortality. Our little dinner table for nine was no longer in Seattle; it was no longer 2016. We were in the timeless space of human story. We could hear the pearls rolling across the table; we even had a sense that Willibel had pulled up a chair and joined us.

What was clear about the present—which came up over the course of the evening—was that it wasn't just happenstance that Cynthia spoke first. She was eager to talk about her grandmother and had been for a long time. Our party heard how Cynthia's mom, in her grief at losing her own mother, had refused to speak about the death, hammering down NO TRESPASSING signs around the topic of Willibel's life ending. Cynthia couldn't access her grief, and so it made the beauty and poetry of her grandmother's life off limits as well. We need to fully grieve someone to fall back in love with them. It's in the acceptance of their loss that we can regain the enchantment of their gifts to us.

We continued around the table, each in turn toasting and lighting a candle—Molly for her elderly neighbor whose funeral she had just attended that day; Jasmine, for a cousin; Brian and Jenna for their grandmothers, after whom they'd named their eldest daughter; Sandy for a beloved aunt; Joe for a childhood friend; Eleanor for a godparent; and me for my father, as I always do. Everyone was fully present: no one checks their Instagram feed during a conversation about death. A group of strangers had each just shared something from the very center of their heart—jobs and accomplishments weren't mentioned, and a profound sense of human connection had been created in a sum total of fifteen minutes.

It was time to eat.

A book is not a dinner party, and I can't prepare every reader a meal. But I do want to extend an important invitation: I invite you to help me change how we talk about death, one conversation at a time.

Something I find fascinating is that we spend so much time, energy, and money focused on self-improvement. We are constantly seeking to be better, to *do life* better. We go to therapy and meditation courses. We go on diets, sign up for CrossFit, and make improvements to our spending. We're a culture obsessed with transformation, and yet we fail to recognize that all transformation includes death and rebirth. The examples are endless, but at the simplest level, consider fall turning into winter and winter turning into spring. In all our striving, we fail to bring death into the conversation, and yet our mortality is the fulcrum of all personal transformation. We don't think about improving our lives in the context of death, and we don't talk about improving our deaths. In this sense I want to underscore that death has many shades: it is the loss of a loved one; the reckoning with that fact that we are all mortal and the sweetness and tragedy that gives life; and it is also the little deaths, the things in us that must die in order for us to grow and become our authentic selves. This book is about giving you and me access to as many shades of death as we need in order to have more freedom and live a more empowered life. Because the way we die in the modern age is broken.

Look no further than the language we use around death—or, rather, the language we avoid. Chyna Wu, a grief specialist/educator, talks about how her friends are constantly urging her not to use the word "death" in her communication materials but to use "passed away" or "went to heaven" instead. "I tell them, if I don't use the words 'death' or 'dying,' who else is going to do it?" she says. She grew up in Hong Kong and feels that Westerners have a particular discomfort with talking about death. "I think it's maybe because Western medicine tends to think it can beat death," she says. "The language is very much about *doing*, things like 'We won't let that happen. We can do this, or do that.'" It's as if we're heroes in an action film, squaring off with an evil foe, and everyone knows the good guy wins in the end. We are doers. We are saviors. If it's us versus death, we will come out victorious.

Of course, this narrative is a myth. And the more we perpetuate it, the more we lose. We're a little messed up about death, to put it bluntly. On the one hand, it's all around us. We flock to dark cable dramas and slow down our cars out of morbid fascination with traffic accidents. But to talk about it with one another? Honestly and openly? Forget it. When we live within this contradiction, we lose the chance for connection, communication, healing, and the richness and value that can come from facing our mortality head-on.

I know this intellectually, and I know it personally. I was born when my father was seventy-two. I was still in elementary school when I realized something wasn't right with him. We were alone in the car one day, and I remember feeling happy that it was just us, that I got my dad all to myself. There was a honeyed light that seemed to emanate from my father. His smile contained an ocean of calm wisdom, and his presence filled me with an otherworldly warmth. Something was strange about the road we bumped along, though as an eight-year-old, I couldn't identify what. It wasn't until a biker raised an angry fist that I realized our Sunday drive had taken a wrong turn. My dad had aimed our old Mercedes sedan away from the auto lanes and onto one of the many bike paths in Black Butte Ranch, entering a forest reserved only for bicycles. The other car traffic was at least a half mile behind.

That incident was a poignant record skip, a pause in the music, which quickly grew to a slow scrape of the needle. The center fell out, though I wasn't aware of how fragile the center had been or for how long. This hole was suitably called "the thirty-six-hour day." It could have been called "the forever day and night." It's also known as Alzheimer's.

For the next five years I saw very little of my father. The many complex reasons for this boil down to one very simple cultural truth: in the United States we don't know how to talk about illness and death with each other and especially with young children. Or, more precisely, we have forgotten. When we step away from one story, my story, and look at the cultural denial of death and our depleted skills to address and discuss terminal illness and loss, the damage is incalculable.

At the most tangible level our reluctance to have this conversation is costing us money every single day. A study from the Mt. Sinai School of Medicine found that 43 percent of Medicare recipients spend more than their total assets—out of pocket—on end-of-life care.[1] Medical care is the number-one factor in US bankruptcies, with end-of-life care expenses—particularly hospital expenses—leading the charges. And although approximately 80 percent of Americans want to die at home, only 20 percent of them do.[2] More than half of us are not getting what we want or what we're entitled to—and we're paying dearly for it. People are bankrupting their families, and for little good reason: most of them don't even *want* expensive, extreme life-prolonging measures, but they haven't talked to their families about their preferences, and no one has asked.

In his recent testimony to Congress, Dr. Atul Gawande, the author of one of my favorite books, *Being Mortal*, detailed the bleak terrain and made a hopeful case for asking patients about their priorities of care as their end draws near:

The most effective and important way to learn these priorities is to ask people about them. The overwhelming majority of the time, however, we don't ask, whether as clinicians or as family members. When we don't ask, the care and treatments we provide usually fall out of alignment with people's priorities. And the result is suffering. But when we do ask, and work to align our care with their priorities, the results are extraordinary . . .

Clinicians ask about their goals for the last phase of their lives less than one-third of the time before they die. Families appear to do little better. And when we do ask, it is generally not until close to the very end.

A number of studies have demonstrated that when people with serious illness have discussed their goals and wishes for their care with their clinician, the outcome is far better. They suffer less, they are more physically capable, and they are better able, for a longer period, to interact with others; their family members were also markedly less likely to experience depression. They enroll in hospice sooner, but they do not die sooner— on average, in fact, they live longer.

Yet how do we act on such information? In recent years politicians urging action have been cast as advocating "death panels." Doctors, hospitals, and insurance companies are often restricted by pressing budgetary needs, the threat of lawsuits, and the current limitations of hospice systems. There is now a Medicare code for end-of-life conversations so that doctors and social workers can bill for it, but early studies indicate that this change has not moved the needle when it comes to the number or quality of conversations we have about death and dying. We rarely even teach doctors and nurses in medical school how to have this conversation.[3]

The medical sphere is not the only place where we're losing money. When people don't talk honestly about their memory loss, for instance, they are not only more vulnerable to making serious financial mistakes but are also more likely to be taken advantage of. Because financial exploitation cases are under-reported (in part because of embarrassment), it's difficult to put a precise number on it, but there may be as many as five million elderly victims of financial exploitation a year in the United States.[4]

And then there's the cost that comes with death itself. Countless grieving family members enter funeral homes and, when plans haven't been discussed in advance, make decisions about coffins and burial based on funeral directors upselling them. In the fog of grief they spend money their family doesn't necessarily have to fulfill a sense of duty that the deceased would never have wanted from them.

The emotional toll of our death avoidance is less tangible but toxic nonetheless. It was Halloween of my thirteenth year when I learned my father died. That night I went out trick-or-treating with my friends without telling anyone what had happened. My mother did not know how to talk about my father's illness, her feelings, or how to provide an opening for us to explore our own pain. We didn't talk about my dad, and as a result we didn't talk much at all. Being unable to talk about my grief or loss with my peers left me feeling depressed, confused, and terribly alone.

A repressed conversation can occupy the same space in the psyche as a secret.

Being in the same room with my surviving family activated the pain, so we avoided each other. A recent study from the National Institutes of Health (NIH) confirms this kryptonite effect, concluding, "Every time you think about a deeply held secret, stress hormones such as cortisol can surge, impacting your memory, blood pressure, and metabolism."[5] The effects of chronic exposure to elevated levels of cortisol include many maladies we suffer today, from high blood pressure to anxiety.[6] Because my family wasn't talking about what was most on our minds, staying away from each other was the safest and healthiest thing we could do.

Chyna Wu was in her early twenties when she lost her parents within three months of one another. Her career as a model was skyrocketing, and she threw her energies into her work in the United States, as if the sea itself could separate her from the grief that lay at home. Depression crept in, but Chyna continued working and didn't talk to anyone about her sadness. Only when she went to college several years later did her suffering surface. She went into the school clinic to treat a minor sickness, and the nurse asked her questions about her family. As Chyna explained the loss of her parents, she broke down. The nurse said, "Oh my god, that's such a traumatic experience. How are you dealing with it?"

"That was the first time I'd heard I'd had a traumatic experience," Chyna says. "It was the tip of the iceberg."

Karen Wyatt, a hospice doctor, remembers how isolated she felt after her father took his own life. None of Karen's friends knew what to say or do—because of the way he died, this was death with a capital D, and it was untouchable. And so they didn't show up for her. The woman who occasionally cleaned Karen's house showed up, though. She appeared on the doorstep one morning when she was not scheduled to work. She had a plant in one hand, a vacuum cleaner in the other, and a determination to offer what help she could. Years later, Karen said, her friends expressed regret that they hadn't come through. In some ways Karen was afflicted with the same barrier as her friends. For years she avoided having any meaningful conversations with her mother and brother. It was too painful. When they finally did talk about it, twenty years after her dad died, it was like a dam broke and they found each other again. Karen experienced several years of closeness with her mother before her mother died. But she lost twenty years. How do you quantify that type of loss?

The Potential

From where I sit, the writing is on the wall. It is time to face the inevitable, and we need a grassroots movement—we need to face our mortality as a village, not as isolated individuals. Funerals, law offices, and hospitals shouldn't be the only places we confront the passing of loved ones. The proper depth of this conversation can't happen when you feel intimidated, overwhelmed, and sad. It happens when you feel comfortable and are not staring down a crisis.

Given the right framing, a "difficult" conversation does not need to be difficult. It can be liberating. It can even be transformative.

It can bring us closer together, put us in touch with our humanity, and remind us what really matters. It can leave us stronger and wiser and bolder than we were before. It can prepare us to have another conversation, when crisis or a terminal diagnosis does arise, that we were not ready to have before.

The studies are clear: open conversation with your family, doctors, and caregivers about your end-of-life wishes results in better care, less suffering, and a longer life. Conversations about death have even proved to make us funnier and more willing to laugh.[7]

If you don't talk about what you want at the end, then you can be sure that you won't get what you want. Picture what you want your final days to be like: Who is around you? Are you in a hospital? Will there be a funeral, and if so, what music is playing and who is speaking? What happens to your body? How do you want to be remembered? Telling your wishes to your friends and family will give them more than the ability to honor you; it will give them the peace of mind to properly grieve you without the weight of doubt and guilt. My friend Lucy Kalanithi, the widow who finished and published her husband's memoir, *When Breath Becomes Air*, recently told me she viewed her conversations with Paul about his impending death as a second wedding vow—a sacred exchange, a vision, and an oath to follow and honor.

Elisabeth Kübler-Ross once said, "It is the denial of death that is partially responsible for people living empty, purposeless lives; for when you live as if you will live forever, it becomes too easy to postpone the things you know you must do." To talk about our own mortality and the mortality of our loved ones is to talk about life. Death is the great mirror. Talking about it does not need to be fearsome or morbid. As my fellow northwesterner Michael Meade so poignantly states, "The role of a fully realized human being is to arrive at the door of death having become oneself."

If we take ownership over our lives and eventual deaths, we can allow others to be powerfully present to our passing and not let it be lost in the chaos of indecision. If doctors and nurses had clear direction from each of us—advance-care directives, clear power of attorney, healthcare proxy—and if our families knew our wishes for the type of care we want at our life's end, if they knew what we want to happen to our body and how we want to be celebrated, the emotional and financial burden would significantly reduce.

By transforming the planning process into an opportunity, a joyful and significant activity that allows us to honor ourselves and our loved ones, we can change the way we die—and the way we live. Death of a close family member or preparing for your own inevitable end can be one of the more daunting experiences we face. This book sets out to make the preparation and planning easier, even beautiful, whether it is an unexpected death or a slow waltz to the finish line.

Please don't mistake my optimism for delusion. I know how hard this terrain is, I know it is not a well-lit path, and yet I believe that every person has the ability to step into these canyons. It is just about how and when, and I hope this book serves as a trail guide.

A Gentle Revolution

"Death is considered such a buzzkill," says Greg Lundgren, a renowned artist who creates beautiful monuments to commemorate the dead. This is not to suggest that death, particularly when it comes to someone young, is not tragic and awful—it is. But Greg points out that although there is no chance to rewrite the story of what's happened, "there can be great ways of using death to create something beautiful. There is opportunity in death to make the world a better place."

In this book you will read stories of how even simply *talking* about death has in fact made the world a better place. It may be in a very relational way, where two family members in the car—or six strangers sitting down for dinner—become closer and more connected through talking about death. It may be in a very personal way, in that embracing conversations about death can ease an individual's anxiety and alter their outlook about life.

Allie Hoffman, an architect of social movements, was in a pretty negative place in her life when she returned to the United

States after many years working in Cambodia. There she had been a constant witness to poverty, rampant sex tourism, and some of the worst parts of humanity. "I had a dark mindset. My mentality was, 'You only have you in this world. People will lie and cheat and betray.' I was very much about the cult of the individual, thinking, 'Don't ever be so naïve to think there's someone you can depend on. Don't ever let yourself be vulnerable.' I was in this tightly wound, intense place."

A year and a half after she returned, her path crossed that of Brittany Maynard—a vibrant twenty-nine-year-old who was dying from an aggressive brain tumor. Brittany had moved her family from California to Oregon in order to use Oregon's right-to-die law, and in her last months she wanted to create a campaign to raise awareness and effect change around the issue. To say she was successful would be an understatement—a video Allie shot of her talking about her decision went hyperviral immediately. For a time Brittany's face was everywhere, and her life and death indeed impacted laws around the right to die. Allie orchestrated the social movement alongside her. Whether or not you agree with what Brittany Maynard wanted, her impact on Allie is irrefutable.

"What Brit taught me," said Allie, "was that when your time has run out, all that matters is love. The love that hurt you, the love that made you ecstatic. It's the greatest human privilege to be loved, and we live in service to it. It was the most profound lesson of my life in a lot of ways. And it took me weeks to sit and stare at the ocean and process. I had wrapped myself tight around this solid set of beliefs that were the antithesis of what it meant to be open and in service to love."

While Allie's conversion was deeply personal, on a larger scale the conversation Brittany opened up with her frankness let loose a dam. The same might be said about the work of Lynette Johnson, who began taking photos of terminally ill children at Children's Hospital in Seattle. When a journalist pitched the piece he wrote about her work to the *Seattle Times*, they declined it based on the notion that people would not want to read about the death of a child over their Sunday breakfast. The story could have ended there, with the prevailing perspective that "people don't want to read about death." But the journalist pitched the story of Lynette's work more widely. When *People* magazine ultimately picked it up, the public's hunger for the conversation was apparent, and Lynette's Soulumination organization exploded. Soulumination is now sixty photographers strong and able to help hundreds of families a year. The good work they are doing for grieving families would never have started if the journalist had not challenged the viewpoint that "people don't want to read about death."

Similarly, the legendary bestseller *Tuesdays with Morrie* (that spawned a made-for-TV movie—Jack Lemmon's final role as Morrie Schwartz—and a play has been staged all over the world for the past two decades) almost did not come to be. It was a *Boston Globe* headline—A PROFESSOR'S FINAL COURSE: HIS OWN DEATH—that caught the eye of *Nightline* senior producer Richard Harris and prompted him to take the profile of the terminally ill Brandeis University professor into Ted Koppel's office.

After reading the story, Koppel instructed Harris to call Schwartz to see if he'd do an interview. For some time, Koppel had wanted to do a *Nightline* story about dying, since he grew up in England and noticed, when he came to the United States as a teenager, Americans were far more reticent to talk about death than the English. So Morrie's willingness to talk about his impending death from ALS, out of step with the American way of death, intrigued Koppel.

Koppel's boss, ABC News president Roone Arledge, was skeptical. "Why do you want to do a program about a guy who is dying? Talk about a downer, " Arledge told Koppel. But Ted went to Boston anyway to interview Morrie. It was so well received—one of the most-watched interviews of Koppel's entire career—that he did two more before Morrie succumbed to the disease.

When Morrie's former student, sports journalist Mitch Albom, saw the first interview by chance, he called Morrie, who invited Albom to visit him. And for the next six months, on each Tuesday, Albom visited Schwartz and collected material for a book he hoped would pay for Morrie's medical expenses. Publisher after publisher rejected it, echoing Arledge's phrase ("too much of a downer"). But just before Morrie died, Albom was able to tell Morrie that the book would be published. *Tuesdays with Morrie* would become the biggest selling memoir in the history of publishing. The book has inspired and uplifted millions upon millions for over twenty years.[8] And yet a tepid response from publishers unwilling to take a risk on death almost blocked this incredible phenomenon.

I hate to come down too hard on anyone who has shied away from this subject. I've personally hosted hundreds of dinners all over the globe to discuss death, loss, and end-of-life preparation, and the clearest thing I have learned is that these conversations rarely happen. It is as if a conspiracy of silence has settled upon us, like a curse on a village, and we have forgotten that we know how to have this dialogue about death. I strongly believe that deep down we know how to face this pain—together—but we need to take the difficult first step and start to talk.

So let's begin.

CHAPTER 2

Extending the Invitation

It was raining so hard on Vashon Island as I stepped off the weathered ferry that it looked like fog. I was nervous. I had no idea how many people would come out in the dead of winter on a stormy night to hear me talk about death. Vashon is home to about ten thousand residents, but they don't leave their houses much, especially in winter, and my talk was one of a dozen or so death-related events happening that week on the island. They were calling it a death festival—how could I say no?

The high school exterior was as clean and bright as a brand-new car, construction completed only months before. The glinting stone pathways intersected with bio-swales of poplar trees and micro-forests of native plants, and the entire estate smelled of deep forest. The façade was thirty feet of crystalline glass, jutting out in an architectural greeting. As the doors opened I was physically embraced by a dozen warm and smiling grandmothers who seemed to be preternaturally excited by my presence. I never met my own grandparents, so this was a new and overwhelming feeling—heartwarming yet uncomfortable. Apparently these elderly ladies were excited about meeting "the death guy."

Atop a massive staircase stood a fourteen-year-old girl dressed in tartans, her hair tied in careful braids. The glowing whiteness of her complexion was accentuated by the dark octopod arms of a bagpipe. Before I knew it, otherworldly sounds filled the massive foyer. Tears pressed against the back of my eyes as I was led into the theatre, but I pushed them back. There was hardly an empty seat, and the sad yearning of the bagpipes mixed with the hundreds of L.L.Bean–clad northwesterners, pushed the pile of tears forward. Self-consciously dabbing at my face, I decided to scratch my existing talk. I asked everyone to close their eyes, as much to gain composure as anything else. After making a joke that I was now going to include bagpipes in my tech rider for future talks, I surprised myself and asked everyone to picture a person they loved deeply who was no longer with us. Although this is a question I always open death dinners with, I'd never used it in a speech-format before. "Once you have that person present in your mind's eye," I said, "visualize a resplendent dinner party. Food is just coming out of the oven, and the smells are over-whelmingly beautiful. The table includes this person who is no longer with us, and it is also filled with a gaggle of their favorite humans. Laughter and mirth are in the air, and we are now just sitting down to a dinner that will be filled with story and humor."

As they opened their eyes, I explained that I am not interested in speaking from a stage, that I feel more comfortable gathering people at the table. I wanted to have us all held in a kind of spell that a great dinner party can cast. And then I asked to hear the names of the dead loved ones who came to mind—not in any order, just spoken out into the theater. Rebecca, Mary, David, Javier, Elizabeth . . . over fifty names were spoken, some whispered, some shot out like a cannon. And this remarkable thing happened, as it always does when we honor our ancestors: time stops, and you suddenly feel that your loved ones happen to be in the room, present, in some way. When you are in the presence of spirit—and I don't mean this in a way that requires faith or even spirituality but rather in the feeling of an old, well-loved cathedral—things have a deeper, slower, more fertile quality.

That evening was one of the best experiences I have had talking to a large or even small group. I hadn't invited them in, really—they'd invited *me*. And then we all seemed to step onto a beautiful boat together, and we took a voyage into death and heart and loss and got to see what we wanted out of the rest of our lives.

A bright May morning in Melbourne, Australia, did not bring the same kind of experience. I stood in a lifeless hotel conference suite at a podium staring out into a sea of about one hundred Aboriginal eyes watching me, stone-like. I was midtalk, and I hadn't stroked a single chord.

As a child I needed to use charm and connection to get noticed and receive love. There was too much drama in our house for it to be offered up without having to work for it. And the love I didn't get at home, I figured out how to get at school. I made sure my teachers loved me and that I was at the center of the most popular students while at the same time being liked by the outcasts. I loved being liked—I still do. Every single thing I had learned as a child, as a young artist, as a restauranteur, and as a dinner host was failing me on the stage that morning.

I blundered on through the statistics about how successful our little project had been in such a short time, sharing our usually popular origin story—that an $11,000 crowdfund had inspired over one hundred thousand dinner parties—with a crowd that remained unimpressed.

There was no point continuing on. My Death Over Dinner (DOD) cofounder, Angel Grant, and I were there to launch DOD in Australia, and it had been a glorious pageant. The project was front-page news for ten days, we were on the flashiest talk shows and all the major radio programs, the Prime Minister asked us to lunch, and we took over a whole episode of Australia's *60 Minutes*, where an entire death dinner was staged and filmed with their biggest movie stars and political personalities. We were punch drunk with the unbelievable success of our launch week. And yet none of that mattered that morning with the fifty Aboriginal leaders, unmoved by my charm.

Just as I'd done on Vashon, I went off script, but this time for the complete opposite reason. I closed my laptop. I came out from behind the podium. I asked the room what people liked and what they didn't like about our project. I was being sincere, and an elderly woman responded immediately.

"The name, it doesn't work for me."

I asked her to elaborate.

"Let's have dinner and talk about death," she said. She screwed up her face a little. "We don't talk about death."

"What do you mean?" I asked.

"We talk about going home."

The room flashed with energy, nods, and slight smiles, a little dance of electricity in everyone's eyes. "Okay," I said. "'Going home'—that's beautiful. What else don't you like about the name?"

"Dinner," she said. "We don't have 'dinner'—that's a gubba word. Our mob, we have a good old feed."

The room was warming up; laughs broke out at a couple tables. I was lost in the maze of new words, but I understood that dinner was on notice, and that a feed was where it was at.

"So what happens at feeds?" I asked.

"Lots of eating and lots of yarns," someone piped up. The room broke open. There it was—the honey you look for when speaking to a group of people.

We were getting somewhere, and my nervous Australian hosts were finally getting color back in their faces. This was the gathering of the week of launch events they had feared most.

I turned to the elderly woman who had spoken first. "So, what if we scrap the name and we build an entirely new project and we call it *A Yarn and a Feed About Going Home?*" That earned a whoop or two from the audience. A few people nodded their heads slowly, taking it in. I saw some silent check-ins crisscross the room as the elders who were present took a nonverbal straw poll.

And the woman replied, "Yeah, that could work."

I left the stage, and we fired up the individual tables to start brainstorming about what it would look like, who would have these dinners, who needed them, how they could be structured, and who would be good partners. By the end of the hour we had gotten the basic framework of an entirely new platform. Before we were seen off that morning with warm embraces, the largest assisted-care facility in Australia had promised to fund the project.

The contrast between Vashon and Australia taught me that there is no one way to extend an invitation to talk about death. Sometimes it's in the language we use, but that's just one factor. Every conversation about death is unique, as is every human heart. DNA, epigenetics, childhood, culture, trauma, ego, self-esteem, hurt, joy, pain—all these factors knit the heart into endless variations. There is always a key; the trick is in finding it.

Gauging Readiness

One of the most frequent questions I'm asked is how someone can make their aging mother/father/grandparent talk to them about their wishes and beliefs surrounding death. Those asking me are usually anxious, and for good reason. Often they feel their loved one is in decline—be it physical or mental—and it's dangerous *not* to talk about it. Either their father will drive a car when he really shouldn't, or he'll continue to manage complicated stock transactions when he really shouldn't. I get it. My primary motivation for writing this book is my conviction that our reluctance to talk about death causes us all manner of pain. And yet my answer to the question is always, always the same: *You cannot make someone talk about death if they're not ready. It won't go well. It just won't.*

Despite the provocative nature of this book's title, I don't ever think it's a good idea to pounce on someone and say, "Hey, let's talk about death." You need to take good care, and you need to take your time, even if you feel time is what you're short on. This is an opt-in conversation.

Court someone first. Create the context in which they'll feel comfortable having the conversation. Cultivate a setting where it's more likely that the person wants to engage. If the person gives resistance, consider how you're asking. How are you bringing up the conversation? Are you coming from a place of expectation, from a "should" mind frame? Is your perspective that you "should" have this conversation or that there's something wrong if you don't? That doesn't work. Period. Remove any attachment you feel to their answer. Take those rejections in stride. Assume you're going to run into prickliness and difficulty. Assume it is going to take honesty, vulnerability, risk, charm, and the best parts of you.

Discussions about death open up such a vulnerable part of somebody, so honor that it might take them a while to open up. Gail Ross remembers that when her mom was dying of cancer, Gail kept raising questions about her end-of-life and burial wishes. Her mom was brought up an orthodox Jew but hadn't been very observant for most of her adult life. How many of the orthodox customs did she want to follow? A plot was waiting for her near her husband's, but he had died decades before, and somehow a funeral in New Jersey didn't seem to fit anymore for this Manhattanite. Gail's mom would say, "I don't want to talk about that now," or "I'm not ready to talk about that," and Gail pulled back. But she would bring it up again, gently: "Mom," she'd say, "I'm going to need to know these things." And little by little, they talked.

I've invited countless people to talk about death with me, and believe it or not, I usually plant the seed over email. Email gives you time as the initiator to think about how you want to ask, and it gives time for the recipient to think about a response and how they feel about entering into that space. You might simply send a link to an article about death and add something like, "I found this interesting. I would love to talk more about this topic with you. Would you be up for it?" If you decide you want to host a dinner party to talk about death, we created a template for Death Over Dinner that you can pull from.

This might be the most unusual dinner invitation I have ever sent, but bear with me. I think we are in for a remarkable experience.

I would be honored if you would take the time to join me for dinner and engage in a conversation about death. This is not meant to be a morbid conversation but instead a very human one where we consider what we want, both in life and during its closure. Through sharing our thoughts and feelings on this subject, we can more readily move through our fears, shed inhibitions, and forge a deeper understanding and connection with our loved ones.

I've extended invitations to talk about death that were declined with an "I'm not ready." Or, in the case of a dinner invite, have gotten responses like "We just don't feel comfortable talking about those issues in that kind of setting." And that's perfectly fair—it's not the right setting—or timing—for everyone. Let the "pass" go without feeling rejected. It's not about you, and you have to watch to make sure none of your ego gets wrapped up in the invitation. You can be the change you want to see by extending the invitation and showing your willingness to talk, but that's really all you can do.

Who, What, Where, Why, and How?

Talking about death is loaded with too many assumptions to count. "It is never the right time," "It will depress my parents," "My spouse is already depressive," "It is too soon after a loss," "It will trigger their anger or rage," "I don't trust myself to be strong or clear in the conversation"—the reasons not to talk are endless. The reason to have the conversation is simple: your life will be better, and so will the lives of your loved ones.

For many of those who tell me their friends or family don't want to talk about death, it turns out they've never asked them. One of the core misconceptions when it comes to talking about death and end of life or even advanced-care planning with our parents is that they are terrified of the conversation. They are closer to death, so you reason that it must be a more fearful topic to them. I understand this logic, but the reality is that it is rarely true. The amount of death humor thrown around my mom's bridge circle would make a funeral director uncomfortable. At many West African funerals the mourners are young women, and the old men sit in the back of the ceremony and tell gallows jokes the entire time, cracking bit after bit about who will be next.

People constantly say to me, "I couldn't possibly talk to him about death—he's dying!" But when someone is dying they often *want* to talk about death—and they feel isolated that no one will engage them in the subject that occupies their mind more than any other. This is why when a nurse proposed having a death dinner at an assisted-living facility, the residents agreed to it only if their kids were invited. "So we can talk about the stuff they don't have the guts to ask us." This is why Steve, who has pancreatic cancer, was adamant that everyone at work know. "There's no point in hiding it," he said. "It's pretty clear I'm sick. I don't want anyone to tiptoe around it." Of everyone in his family, he is the most eager to talk about his illness, the fact that it's terminal, and what it feels like to live in that space.

People also often ask about children. Should children be invited to the discussion? The short answer is: it depends. If they are curious, if they express interest in talking about death, then I would welcome that. And certainly if there has been a death around them or if they are asking a lot of questions about it, they should be met where they are and with honesty. I dig much deeper into this concern on pages 101–107.

I also think it's vital and enriching to have this conversation with those who *don't* necessarily share your views. The key is, one, framing the discussion with curiosity and respect and, two, recognizing that the commonalities we all have as humans far overshadow our differences. Never was I reminded of this more than when Angel and I went to Nashville for a death dinner with former Senate Majority Leader Bill Frist. The table was full of Nashville legends like Vince Gill and Amy Grant, but that's not what made me nervous; rather, I was nervous because I am from the Northwest, where we are known for our liberal politics and our less-than-evangelical interpretations of spirituality. This was my first death dinner in the South. What if the dinner ended in a clash of politics? What if I was told I would burn in hell because I have a less-than-conventional relationship with god and spirit?

What I learned that night is that the conversation about death dips way below the waterline of politics or faith. It was not a divisive evening in the least. Talking about death does not equal talking about or weighing each other's faith; it is not a moralistic conversation. We are all children in the face of death. And by that I mean there is an innocence and a willingness to make deep connections across cultural, political, racial, and gender divides. What was created that night over the course of three hours was a powerful sense of family. Everyone at the table shed tears, which allowed me to rewire my thinking about southern men and their ability to show emotion. Bill Frist reflected how the simple questions had "stripped away inhibitions. People need to talk about death. The conversation is like a top being blown off a boiling pot."

A Word on the Table

I am biased in favor of talking about death over dinner, as the dinner table is the most important crucible of culture we have as humans. Cooking and eating together were transformative in our evolution from ape to human; the table is our cocoon and chrysalis. We made the evolutionary leap thanks to cooking. Apes chew seven hours a day—a diet of roots and fruit requires a huge belly and incredibly strong jaws. When we began cooking over fire we literally began to outsource that big belly, as cooking concentrates calories and makes food more digestible. Humans chew twenty-four minutes a day on average, and because we don't need those strong muscular jaws, they thinned. The big belly turned into a big brain, filling the space left behind by the jaw. Dinner is in fact at the very core of who we are.

The table hasn't always held this pull for me. I spent much of my youth in front of Super Mario Brothers and a bowl of cereal. I didn't learn the importance of the dinner table until I was in my late teen years and flew to Maine to live with my half-sister, Wendy, in an idyllic coastal village. Twenty years my senior, Wendy was married to a brilliant doctor, and the two of them were raising a feisty nine-year-old son. Wendy went to the co-op every other day and farmer's markets when they were open, buying bushels of gorgeous produce, pasture-raised meat, local cheese, and always a healthy amount of French wine. She cooked dinner every night, spending hours in the kitchen, clearly in love with the entire process of shopping, cooking, and providing nourishment for her family. I was entranced and would spend most afternoons perched at the kitchen counter talking philosophy and spirituality and asking questions about her cooking techniques. I had never experienced anything remotely akin to that dinner ritual. We cracked a bottle of good wine, tore apart handmade bread, and talked about our day. It was the oldest, most simple ritual we have, and I was completely in love. I felt seen, understood. We argued, debated, laughed, and talked about sex, drugs, the mundane, and the spiritual.

When you talk over a meal it's the food that speaks first. There's a unique aroma when food has been cooked with love and care. It isn't one note but rather something harder to define. It anchors you when you experience it. This is the power of a home-cooked meal, of bread just out of the oven. When you carefully prepare a meal, taking the time to select the ingredients and then cooking even a humble meat dinner, the smells speak to our central nervous system and tell us we're safe. Sara Williams started a Death Café—a club, of sorts, of people who gather to talk about death while enjoying everything from pastries to Mexican food—outside Chapel Hill, North Carolina. As she put it: "It's always good to be eating while you're talking about death. It tells you you're still alive."

"Breaking bread" together is synonymous with connecting with one another, or, as in the Eucharist, with something more spiritual. As the medical director of Vitas Hospice recently said, "There was a rather famous death dinner. It included a well-known radical thinker and his twelve disciples. He told them he would be dying soon and gave them detailed instructions about what to do with his body and how to spread his teachings when he was gone."

Political enemies will sit over a meal together, and crucial moments in history have transpired over a well-laid table. In June of 1790 Thomas Jefferson, James Madison, and Alexander Hamilton met over dinner to sort out the financial future of the United States and determine the location of our nation's capital. The table has been the smallest, most effective engine of culture for thousands of years. It was at Gertrude Stein's table where Hemingway met Picasso and where the art movement known as Cubism was first sparked. The Tuxedo Park dinners in upstate New York led to the invention of radar, arguably the most crucial piece in the World War II victory. The discovery of oxygen was debated and refined at the monthly dinners of the Lunar Men. Virginia Woolf and John Maynard Keynes gathered with friends—later to be known as the Bloomsbury Group—around the table every week, giving rise to not only modern literature but also the beginning of Keynesian economics, the backbone of our economy. If we go further back, we can credit the food-laden Greek symposiums of Socrates and Plato as the birthplace of democracy and our justice system.

Regardless of its grand and somewhat secret history, the dinner table has been the heart of family life for as long as we have had supper. It is where we come to know each other and where we come to know ourselves. It is where we learn how to converse, it is often where we learn about morality, and it can be where we first experience injustice. However good or bad our experience, the dinner table is a teacher. Despite the fact that dinner has shaped history and continents, individual dinners thrive on modesty.

If you choose to discuss death over a meal, I have a few words of advice. First, keep it simple. If the food preparation is too onerous or stressful, your guests will feel it and your attention will be elsewhere. Second, engage their help. Nothing breaks the ice more than people working together, even if it's in as basic a task as setting the table. Third, begin the evening with the toast to a loved one who has passed, and encourage everyone to discuss the first person to enter their mind and to keep it to about a minute each. Pick three to four prompts from this book to use, but don't get too ambitious—it's not a competition. Choose the prompts that you feel will best speak to your guests, but don't feel wedded to them if the conversation moves elsewhere. If the mood becomes emotional, let it. Notice and resist the urge to placate any sadness that comes up. However, if it feels that you are losing control of the evening, be ready to redirect the conversation with a lighter-natured prompt. Finally, before ending the evening, complete an appreciation in the round, where you express something you admire about the person sitting to your left. This practice offers a warm finish to the evening, and I say much more about this in *How do you end a conversation about death?* on pages 216–221.

The Metaphorical Table

While I believe in the power of the dinner table, I also believe you can create this sense of safety and have meaningful conversations about death over takeout, beers, or during a walk around the neighborhood. You can have it in a high school auditorium in Vashon or in a conference room in Melbourne. The dinner table won't be the most practical or even the best emotional space for everyone. For many the proposition of answering questions in an impromptu way at a dinner inspires nausea. Some will prefer to write their responses and to take weeks to think them through. Others will prefer to talk about death only abstractly . . . at least at first.

Books have long been powerful conversation starters, and so you might suggest reading a book like *When Breath Becomes Air*, *Tuesdays with Morrie*, or *Smoke Gets in Your Eyes*, the latter by mortician Caitlyn Doughty and then talking afterward about some of their themes. If a book feels like too much or if the person you want to talk with really isn't a reader, send an article—an emotional "think" piece—that might touch on his personal experiences. If she's a veteran, for instance, send an article about a soldier facing his mortality. If he's religious, send an article that appeals to his spiritual beliefs. The way in will be different for everyone.

Movies and theater can also be a gentle entry point. When we passively watch a film, we're emotionally very involved. There's a science to this: we have mirror neurons that literally mirror what someone projects to us. Elizabeth Coplan, a playwright who uses theater as an entryway for talking about death and grief, talks about how when we enjoy theater, we're working from the right sides of our brains—the creative and brainstorming parts. Our left brain is our analytical side. When it comes to death, you *want* the two working together; you want to be feeling and thinking. Art can help bridge the divide. Elizabeth once watched *Million Dollar Baby* alongside an octogenarian who refused to talk about death. For the few who don't already know, the movie's ending involves the assisted suicide of a quadriplegic dependent on a ventilator. After the movie the octogenarian told Elizabeth, "If I were in that position, I'd want someone to do that for me." To him this did not count as talking about death. And yet of course he was.[1]

While art can serve as an effective entry, so can questions that are more abstract, like: What do you want to be remembered for? What do you want your grandchildren to tell their grandchildren about you? What would your epitaph be? Answer the questions yourself as well. When you open up and show your own vulnerability and willingness to talk, you open up their door too. You might say something like, "You know, I was thinking about how Grandma Mary was always so welcoming and hospitable. Anyone could stay with her, whenever they wanted. I've tried to be like that because it's important. I want my grandkids to remember me that way." Then leave it be. If they don't respond with their own desires, that doesn't mean they're not thinking about it. Give them time. You are planting seeds.

How to Use This Book

As you already see, this is an unusual book. As such, there are some things you need to know about what you're holding—literally and metaphorically.

First, this isn't a book that needs to be read in order. There is no narrative arc except for the ever-present arc of life and death. No spoilers. Some people do appear several times, but you don't need to have read their first mention to appreciate the others.

Second, this isn't a book that should be read in one sitting. It's not a long book, but I consider it a thinking book, a meditative book. If you move on too quickly, you run the risk of covering too much emotional and intellectual territory. The stories took five years to discover, so I suspect it should take at least a couple of weeks to digest them.

You can read this book again and again. The words on the page won't change, but you will. And if you use it to facilitate a dinner, your relationship with it will be different from if you're reading through it solo. I still actively practice beginner's mind with every dinner or conversation I host. I act as if I am coming to the topic fresh, led only by my own vulnerability.

This book will piss you off. I don't know where. That will be different for everyone. You might come across a topic that just does not feel relatable to you. Or one that feels it's taking a leap too far. Or one that hits you so hard with its resonance that you need to look away. That's fair. Just skip it. Maybe you'll come back to it. Maybe not. There's no judgment here.

You may feel aggravated that this book doesn't offer a bulleted list of answers. Maybe you came across it in the self-help section, whether in a bookstore or online, and you want conclusions drawn, prescriptions written, a literary "pill" to take. You want black and white, right and wrong. And in some cases there *are* answers. I've talked to many people who know their stuff, and there are clear parameters around some topics—like how to talk to kids about death or what to consider when someone is deep within the throes of grief. There is guidance, but there are questions that remain. The stories in this book are of both well-known and anonymous people, and they are offered to give you ideas, to provoke your left and right brain at once, but they are not here to provide definitive answers. They are meant to give you comfort with the notion that there are no clear answers to some of these questions. As Wendell Berry wrote, "It may be that when we no longer know what to do, we have come to our real work, and when we no longer know which way to go, we have begun our real journey. The mind that is not baffled is not employed. The impeded stream is the one that sings."

Despite the necessary ambiguity of advice in this book, there is one solid, golden rule that gets me through every difficult conversation about death—or sex or drugs—with family, strangers, friends, lovers, and even sworn enemies. I know that I need to identify and say the things I am afraid of saying. This is the tried-and-true method: to meet each person with radical vulnerability in these hard topics. Honesty and vulnerability are contagious.

THE PROMPTS

Each chapter that follows is stated as a question. These are questions I have used in thousands of conversations, and they have come from a variety of different sources and been polished and clarified again and again. Though it is obviously not a complete list, these are the questions I suggest you pull from when talking about end of life with loved ones, friends, patients, and strangers.

If you had only thirty days left to live, how would you spend them? Your last day? Your last hour?

The train sped along from Seattle to Portland on a spectacular summer morning, following the track along the waterways of the lower Puget Sound. One of my daughters lived in Portland at the time, so I found myself on the train frequently. Like most of us, I don't seek out conversations with strangers while traveling, which is unfortunate, as I have had transformative moments when I decide to engage and treat fellow passengers as fellow humans.

That day the train was crowded, and I didn't have the option of keeping my distance. I found myself at a table with two women—both physicians and both of whom had left the conventional healthcare system because the chaos had disgusted and beaten them down. They didn't know one another before that crowded train ride but weren't surprised when they'd so quickly found common ground.

I asked them what piece of our healthcare system was most broken? They both immediately answered, speaking at the same time: "How we die. End of life." This was in 2012, and how we die in the United States was not front-page news. (Atul Gawande's *Being Mortal* wasn't published until two years later.) I was taken aback and asked for more information. I quickly learned the two devastating statistics I mentioned in Chapter 1: that end-of-life care is the number-one factor in US bankruptcies and that although 80 percent of Americans want to die at home, only 20 percent do.

I asked them if they agreed that how we end our lives is one of the most important—and costly—conversations Americans aren't having. They did.

Then I asked: If I created a national campaign called Let's Have Dinner and Talk About Death, did they think I would find support from physicians, insurance companies, patients—essentially everyone? "Definitely," they said. "This has to happen." The three of us clasped hands in a quasi-kumbaya moment, and a fellowship was born, even though I haven't seen those two doctors again since.

I tell this story because it represents the heart of the Death Over Dinner experience, and it inspired this prompt. When we think—really *think*—about how we want to die, and when we talk with others about it, we have much more of a chance of making it happen. I don't use this prompt in every death dinner, but it's possibly the most important. If you only had thirty days left to live, how would you spend them? What would your last day look like? Who is around you?

Of the many things these questions evoke, perhaps the most important sentiment is that you only die once. We carefully consider and plan our weddings and our children's births, and we recognize these moments as major transitions. To deny our end of life the same level of consideration denies a tremendous part of us, perhaps the most important part: that we are in fact mortal. We might not be able to control how our final days or hours look or what they feel like, but we can do our best to make sure our wishes are communicated and honored.

Some people say they want to die alone, which is what I used to say. I thought I'd like to wander off into the woods when my time came and pass away quietly without being a burden to anyone, as cats are known to do. But the first time I answered this question out loud, at a death dinner, what came out of my mouth wasn't the noble loner narrative. It was clear to me that I wanted my two daughters—and no one else—to be with me. I could see that it wouldn't be a burden to them but a gift to all three of us. That realization changed the way I parent from that moment forward. I realized I had kept my children at a "safe" distance from many of my emotions and experiences, and because of this, they didn't feel emotionally safe in my presence. There are certain things we don't share with our children, but our emotions, our depth of feeling, is not something to take off the table.

Thinking about what we want for our last days and moments illuminates, then, what we love and value about life. People talk about wanting to be with their dogs, eating chocolate cake, or staring at the ocean. "I imagine shrooms will be involved in the last couple of days," my friend Joe answered thoughtfully. "Then, on the last day, I want to eat a huge stack of big, fluffy pancakes. And then I want to have sex."

I used the "thirty days" prompt at one of my first death dinners, and I was particularly nervous because among the attendees were the president of United Healthcare, the CEO of Weight Watchers, the CEO and COO of TEDMED, David Ewing Duncan from the *New York Times*, and the vice president of Wellness at Walmart. I am not easily shaken by a guest list, but this felt like a terrible way to preview our new endeavor.

One of the guests was Olivia Shaw, who pushed her chair back and easily grabbed the attention of the entire room. Thus far I had been the only one to stand when speaking, so I felt my blood pressure rise. Olivia looked everyone carefully in the eye and said, plain as day, "I don't know about the rest of you, but during my last breath I am going to be buck naked, on top of my man, having the wildest orgasm of my life."

The room exploded in laughter.

The dam had broken, and for the rest of the evening a sense of profound permission pervaded the table.

Thanks to Olivia I have approached every dinner since with a glint in my eye, making space for the profane, the bawdy, the human. Death, dying, and end of life need humor and honesty. Imagine a birth without joy, tears, and laughter. When we treat death as too precious, we kill the humanity of the experience, and this is true no matter whether you are convening over dinner or in fold-up chairs on your front porch.

⌒

Maria felt a great sense of dread leading up to the death dinner, this time she was hosting her family. It was her third death dinner. She'd been to one at my apartment, and she'd hosted one with a group of friends. Her first foray as a hostess had gone well, and she recognized how bonding and meaningful the experience had been for every guest. How could she *not* host a death dinner with her parents and sister? When it came to issues of life and death, other than her husband, these were the people she was most closely bound to. But the stakes felt much higher because, well, family.

For dinner she kept to her sister's request, which was to order pizza from a nearby restaurant that was her sister's favorite. She filled out the meal with a homemade vegetable soup, salad, and plenty of wine. Maria's husband settled their kids upstairs with sandwiches and a movie, and with the help of a strong cocktail, Maria felt almost ready for the evening.

It did not begin well. Maria's sister, Constance, and her husband showed up with their three-year-old and five-year-old, and Maria couldn't help but say in surprise, "Oh! I didn't realize you were bringing the kids." Constance's face reddened, and so Maria quickly jumped in with, "Don't worry. It will be fine. We'll put them upstairs with their cousins to watch a movie."

Constance took a while to recover. She hadn't been looking forward to the dinner in the first place, that was clear, and felt understandably put out by the fact that her kids hadn't been expected. "You could have been explicit about it," she told Maria. "I didn't know."

"It'll be fine!" Maria said. "Relax! It's all good."

But Maria still had work to do. Constance's husband made jokes about how he was going to check the football scores throughout the dinner and hoped that was okay. Maria's dad, Peter, said, "No, you won't"—lightly, but not quite *that* lightly. Maria's mom, Jo, who hated discord of any kind, tried painfully hard to be jovial. Constance was still red and clearly upset about the misunderstanding with the kids. Maria was edgy, worrying that the night had gone irretrievably off course and was also now worrying about whether they'd have time for a meaningful conversation during the length of just one kids' movie.

And so the evening started. Everyone eased in a little bit with the honoring of a loved one who had died. Then, when Maria asked how you would want to spend your last thirty days, your last day, your last hour, things got *really* interesting.

Jo said she wouldn't want to know.

"Okay, Mom, but pretend that you *do* know," Maria pressed.

"I know, but I'm saying I don't want to."

"That's not the way the game is played," Peter said.

Jo delved a bit deeper and talked about how she would spend the last thirty days going for walks with her friends, playing mahjong, and spending time with her kids and grandkids.

The conversation morphed to how people had answered the question at various death dinners.

"Sex comes up a lot," Elliott, Maria's husband, offered. Like Maria, this was his third death dinner. "A lot of people want to go out that way." *Oh god*, Maria thought. *Elliott brought up sex in front of my parents.* She'd been prepared to be vulnerable and have a deep discussion with her family, but not about *sex*. She looked nervously around the table to see if everyone was as mortified as she was.

Jo looked thoughtful. "You know, my dad died that way," she said.

"WHAT?" Maria asked. Peter, Jo's husband, echoed the surprise.

"Well, I mean, technically he died in the hospital. But he had the stroke that sent him there during sex, and he never woke up." Jo went on to explain that in the month preceding his death her father had suspected it was coming. And not in a completely arbitrary way. He had atrial fibrillation, an abnormal heart rhythm, and had had a small stroke. When Jo took him to the doctor, further testing was recommended. But he didn't want any of it. He'd been born in 1915 and had grown up in a tiny Texas town. He'd seen several family members die of typhoid, and he'd fought in World War II. He wore a felt fedora everywhere he went and lived a life of simplicity and decency. If Harry Truman had a mumbling Texan accent instead of a Missouri one, he'd be a perfect stand-in for Maria's grandfather. He called his wife of over fifty years "Mama," and she called him "Daddy." He was a devout Methodist and believed that when your time was up, it was up.

Jo remembered getting into a rare argument with him during one of their last visits because he kept bringing up death. "Stop talking about dying, Dad," she'd pleaded. "You're not going to die."

A few weeks later he turned to his wife in the middle of the night. "Mama," he said, "Do you want to make love?"

And that was that. The dinner table was astounded.

"I can't believe," Peter inserted, "that in fifty years you never told me this."

"That is so gross," said Constance, but she smiled.

"That's awesome," said Maria. She loved that her sweet grandfather had ended his life this way—it was just so fitting.

And the dinner progressed beautifully from there.

When it was Peter's turn he said, "It's strange to think of this now, I wouldn't go there when I thought I really might have just thirty days." Nearly twenty years prior, when he was fifty-three, he'd been diagnosed with colon cancer. The week in between the diagnosis and the surgery—when he would learn the extent to which the cancer had already spread—felt interminable. Based on that news, he would either have thirty days, a year, or the chance to still live out thirty more years of life. Of the many conversations he had that week with Jo, his parents, and his kids, he didn't talk about how he would want to spend his time if he had just a month. He didn't want to think about it.

Happily, the news from the surgery was good, and after a long period of chemotherapy Peter made a full recovery. In the comfort of that recovery the question of how he would spend the end of his life felt like safer ground to tread, and he—along with most people who have confronted a possible terminal illness—found himself returning to the subject frequently over the years. The night of the death dinner Peter pulled his twenty years' worth of fragmentary thoughts together.

"I would spend the first week reading," he said. "I'd want to study what the best thinkers had to say about spirituality, death, existence. I wouldn't read original scripture—I'd read summaries or books referring to scripture. Then I would read material on Buddhism, on Judaism. I'd want to know what other religions said about the meaning of life. I'd want the chance to expand my thinking, to delve into inquiry in a way I haven't made space in my life to do.

"Then I'd travel—by myself," he said. "I'd want to go alone into parts of the world that are unfamiliar to me." Many people say they would want to see the world before they died, but that wasn't Peter's focus; rather, though Peter isn't a Buddhist and had never studied it, he naturally gravitated toward wanting an experience of nonattachment. "I'd want to just get outside of myself, to get rid of all my stuff, my own upbringing and relationships and connections. I'd want to become completely anonymous and get into the unfamiliarity of the rest of the world before I leave it."

But then he'd return home, he explained, and do the exact opposite. He'd want to spend a week going through family photos, reflecting on his past and reliving his life. He'd want music from the sixties, seventies, and eighties playing to put him back in that time and place.

In the last week or so he would want to spend time with his children and grandchildren, talking about what he'd studied, talking about what he'd seen in the world, talking about the life he'd lived. He wouldn't want to leave any of the philosophy or reflection unspoken, unshared.

Finally, he'd want to spend the last days just with Jo, to whom he'd been married for almost fifty years. "At that point," he explained, "there wouldn't be a need to say much. We'd have said it all and would just sit together."

What I find interesting about Peter's approach is that it's almost like he viewed his last month from a director's point of view and wanted to take the long shots, the broad views of the landscapes before narrowing in for the close-ups and the fade to black. A month, split equally into *This is life, writ large* and *This is your life*.

Peter had twenty years to ask himself these questions when he did not have the feeling of standing on a precipice. When you are on that precipice, it feels different. Sometimes, like Jo, you don't want to know the end is coming. Sometimes doctors don't want to tell you. This begins to explain why only one in sixteen cancer patients can accurately describe their prognosis.[1] Doctors are human, and so are patients. And we're all scared in the specter of hastened mortality.

"I have extraordinary empathy and compassion for how that happens," said Alexandra Drane, a respected entrepreneur in the healthcare field, "because as somebody who has had a diagnosis of a brain tumor, it's so terrifying to cognitively look at your own end of life."

Alex also has enormous empathy with doctors on the subject. "When would you ever want to go into work and have on your to-do list *I'm going to tell them bad news*? Every day you would prioritize telling them something else. That doesn't excuse doctors for not having these conversations, but it explains how hard it really is. Added to that, a lot of patients are sending out signals that 'I don't want to know anything this bad.' It's more understandable how it happens. But it's still inexcusable."

The reason Alex is so passionate about this isn't because of her own diagnosis—she is now tumor-free—but because of how very traumatic the last thirty days were with her sister-in-law, Za. It took years for her to be able to unpack the experience and the role that not talking about death had on the end of Za's life.

In the days leading up to Alex's wedding to Antonio, Za's brother, there was great anticipation and excitement. Members of Antonio and Za's family flew in from Italy for what was to be a phenomenal celebration on New Year's Eve. During that time before the wedding Za experienced some excruciating headaches. While others took care of Za's daughter, then a toddler, Za had a hard time getting out of bed and wasn't herself. Among the cries of "pull up your socks, Za—your brother's getting married" there was also a thrumming worry. On the day of the wedding someone suggested Za might be dehydrated, so her husband took her to their local hospital right outside of Boston—hopefully an IV would set her right. But she and her husband didn't show up for the wedding. As Alex and Antonio exchanged their vows, Za's head was scanned and her doctors grew alarmed. They transferred her by ambulance to a renowned Boston teaching hospital. When Alex and Antonio called the next day, Za's husband could barely speak with the shock of how sick his wife had become so quickly. The newlyweds postponed their honeymoon and drove to the hospital instead.

At this point Za had lost the ability to speak English and was speaking only Italian, her first language. As Antonio went into her room to try to translate, Alex spoke to the surgeon sitting outside Za's room and looking at the computer.

"What are you looking at?" Alex asked.

"A scan of her head," he said. "It's glioblastoma, and I think it's stage four."

Alex walked outside and called her mom on her cell phone, asking her to look up what it meant. (This was in the days before smartphones.) She learned that it meant the worst—it was literally one of the worst diagnoses you can receive, a diagnosis that came with just a 5 percent chance of living more than five years.

While Za had surgery right away and started radiation, no one in the family other than Alex knew Za's prognosis and what it meant. In fact, they pointedly didn't want to know.

A few months later they learned that the radiation hadn't worked. A second surgery was immediately recommended, which now, looking back, makes Alex furious. "If they'd had a palliative care specialist involved," she said, "they would never have told her to do it. Never ever ever. Why would you ever go back into someone's brain?" Especially when, as Alex and Za's doctors knew, there really was no hope.

All the while it was weighing heavily on Alex that Za didn't know her true prognosis. She talked to a social worker at the hospital, explaining, "What if she wants to write a series of letters to her daughter? For her sixteenth birthday, for her wedding day? What if she wants to prepare her daughter now for the fact that she's dying? This is not okay."

The social worker said, "You can't make that decision for her. What you can say is 'Za, if this was me, I'd want to know everything that was happening.'"

Alex vividly remembers finally sitting down with Za, who "didn't know how to have the conversation, and I didn't know how to do it. And she said, 'I don't want to talk about it,' and I said 'okay.'"

"It took months . . . years . . . before the water ran clear," said Alex. "I was so muddy about how Za died. It's so clear now that we all had PTSD. She was tortured on some level. It just takes time to be able to breathe again and think with clarity again. And once we could, what I couldn't get past was how did we let that happen? How did we let her have the worst death possible? How is this all right?

"We never gave her the great honor of knowing her diagnosis and knowing her choices. And if we had had those conversations about death earlier and not because of any particular situation— just naturally as a family, before her diagnosis, we would have handled things differently." Alex's experience of Za's illness and death led in part to the creation of Engage with Grace. The organization's mission is to improve the end-of-life experience and to get people talking and asking each other a series of questions about their end-of-life priorities.

There is one part of the end of Za's life about which, when Alex looks back, she feels relief instead of regret. When the end of Za's life was near, her family took the ICU doctor aside and told him that they wanted to take Za home.

Her doctor said no, firmly, that her case was much too complicated. Alex, who had been assertive and verbal through Za's illness, froze in the face of this doctor saying no. But Antonio didn't back down, and neither did Za's husband, John. "No," they said, "we're taking her home." And they did.

The next day, as Za lay in a bed in the house she grew up in, surrounded by familiar smells and sounds, her two-year-old daughter crawled in next to her and nestled her head against her mother's neck. Her daughter had avoided skin-on-skin contact with her mother while she was in the hospital bed, seemingly overwhelmed by the drama of the medical ward. For the first time in over a week Za opened her eyes, fully woke up, and locked her gaze with her daughter's. She closed them again for good and died the next day.

That little toddler, Allessia, would for years ask her family to tell her about the last time her mother opened her eyes. What a gift—to mother, to daughter, to brother, to husband, to sister-in-law—that Za was able to spend her last night at home with her family and that the last image she laid her eyes on was the face of her daughter. Za's illness and death are tragic, but Alex remains so grateful for that last beautiful moment of peace they all witnessed.

What foods do you remember a departed loved one cooking for you?

When I asked author Tim Ferriss for a recipe from someone he loved who had died, Tim sent a simple bedtime tonic—apple cider vinegar, honey, hot water—which he prepares religiously. Every time the sweet-sour snap of steam hits his nose he thinks of one of his mentors, Dr. Seth Roberts, and his eyes begin to grow heavy. Ferriss is perhaps the best-known self-experimenter of our time, synonymous with the concepts of biohacking and personal optimization. Many of his adventures take you down complex rabbit holes, but this simple concoction of three ingredients has proven to be the best curative for insomnia he has found and the most evocative of a relationship he held dear.

The trick with food is that the baroque, the overwrought, is never the most memorable. If you ask people about their most memorable meal, and I have asked hundreds this simple question, you will never get a story about a dinner at NOMA or some other Michelin-starred restaurant. M. F. K. Fisher wrote, "Gastronomy is and always has been connected with its sister art of love." People remember meals where love was present. Our relationship to food shares a map with our personal history of friendship, fellowship, and love. I am not just talking about romantic meals shared on the banks of the Seine; the table feeds off the boisterous love of friends and family. The table likes to overflow.

When we think about, make, and eat food that those who have died once made for us, it's a form of remembrance that speaks to all our senses at once. A bite of a doughy cinnamon bun, the crackle of latkes, the texture of a tender brisket, the scribbled notes in the margins of a stained cookbook—all are imprints of memory, of a relationship that, although perhaps not formed over food, unfolded with food as the witness.

When Jenna was fourteen her grandfather died of a stroke. On his last visit, as was his habit, he had filled Jenna's family's freezer with applesauce he'd made from the apples in his orchard. No one but Jenna really liked the applesauce—her siblings found the texture too chunky; her parents found the flavor too sweet. Though a pretty self-obsessed fourteen-year-old, Jenna found it deeply meaningful that her grandfather was still able to nourish and care for her after his death. She rationed every last jar of that applesauce, which had been carefully marked in her grandfather's hand with the date it was made. With each bite she imagined him peeling the apples with his arthritic hands, chopping, stirring, carefully jarring. She made all but one of those jars last until a year after he'd died.

The last jar of applesauce Jenna decided to leave. She didn't want to know she was taking the last bite of something her grandfather had made. She doesn't know what happened to that jar in the decades that have passed. But every fall Jenna collects apples, peels them with her daughters, slices them, and makes applesauce. And every fall she tells her daughters stories about her grandpa.

For celebrated Spanish chef José Andrés, paella is arguably the most important dish he makes. Many consider it the national dish of Spain, and it is deeply tied to his personal story as a chef. However, now when he makes the dish, he thinks of a boy named David. José met sixteen-year-old David at the DuPont farmer's market in Washington, DC, where they began a hunt to get David to eat more vegetables. David had an aggressive brain cancer and needed to change his diet so he'd be strong enough to fight the disease. "Together we shopped around the market and picked ingredients for me to show him how to make a paella filled with vegetables that he would like," José said. That evening they cooked the paella together in José's backyard.

"David was so passionate about cooking and the ingredients—he even spoke to his food just like I do," said José. "He had a true appreciation for food and for life. Despite his illness and his suffering, he never wanted special treatment and was always giving back. When asked what he wanted for Christmas, he said to give his presents to the other sick kids whom he had met in the hospital. When the Make-A-Wish Foundation granted him a wish, he said to give it to somebody else."

David and José remained good friends in the years following that day. "When I visited him in the hospital not long before he surrendered to his battle in the spring of 2012, he kept telling me how he couldn't wait to get better so that he could cook and eat again. It was truly amazing how food and cooking kept him alive."

At David's funeral, José remembered, "Hundreds and hundreds of loved ones gathered to share stories and feast on paella, the very same kind of paella we made in my backyard the first time we met. I thought to myself that this was a party, and I was so happy because I knew in my heart it was how David would've wanted it to be. Friends and family, together, united over one meal. When I go I want it to be like that. I will always carry David's spirit with me. He was a selfless, passionate young man, and he still inspires me every single day. Every time I make this vegetable paella I smile and remember David, and I think of how lucky the angels in heaven are to have a chef like him."

José's culinary skills have often been lauded in the press, but his cooking made headlines for a different reason in the fall of 2017. Frustrated by the president and other US nonprofits' response to the hurricane that devastated Puerto Rico, José chartered his own boats and headed to the islands to serve the hungry. He figured out a way to serve millions of warm meals, including paella and sandwiches. As one report said of his efforts, "No other single agency—not the Red Cross, the Salvation Army nor any government entity—has fed more people freshly cooked food since the hurricane, or done it in such a nurturing way." It seems to me it is just what David would have done if he could have.

Kathleen Flinn is perhaps the closest thing we have to a modern-day Julia Child. After a layoff from her corporate job at age thirty-six, Kathleen Flinn packed her bags and headed for Paris to fulfill a lifelong dream—to enroll at Le Cordon Bleu culinary school. She chronicled her stories in a hilarious and sumptuous *New York Times* bestseller, *The Sharper the Knife, the Less You Cry*. These days she works on teaching people across the socioeconomic spectrum to cook at home.

Several years ago her mom joined her for a segment of a book tour, and the two had breakfast at a North Carolina café. "The waitress dropped off a pair of huge, flaky biscuits, a chilled ramekin packed with soft, sweet butter, and a small bowl of dark jam. As Mom and I chatted, she spread the butter and jam on her biscuit. Then she took her first bite and her eyes grew wide. She put down the biscuit and began to cry."

Kathleen was alarmed and asked what was wrong, but her mom just dug in her purse for a tissue. Minutes passed before she could explain what had come over her. "It's just that this tastes just like my dad's jam," her mom said quietly, dabbing her eyes. Kathleen's mom had tried for years to replicate his jam, but it was never right. Kathleen's grandfather had never written down any specifics, and no one could capture the flavor. "It made me miss him so much all of a sudden," she said.

Kathleen understood: she had lost her own father when she was just thirteen. She had missed him every day of her life since, particularly during the great celebrations in her life—her graduation, her wedding. "If I could have one brief conversation with him now, I'd ask the secret to his chicken and dumplings," Kathleen said. She has been trying to make them the way he did for more than thirty years. "So irrational, but somewhere, my heart believes that if I can get that recipe right," she said, "I can have him back, just for a moment. Just for one bite."

Food—and the long memory that comes with certain dishes, or flavors—is wrapped together in the way we care for others too. It is the reason we drop food off when we need to do *something*, when we want to show our love. Food is the way we nourish the body and one another, and so when someone stops eating altogether, to stand by and do nothing feels iniquitous. James Beard award–winning chef Jody Adams's family gathers together every year on Cape Cod to eat masses of corn, lobster, and tomatoes. But one year her father couldn't eat much more than soup. Cream of mushroom was his favorite, and so that's what she made. "By the second week we were back in Boston, and I had to spoon-feed him," she said. The third week he kept slipping in and out of consciousness. "As I sat on the side of his bed, fighting back tears and holding a bowl of cold soup, my mother touched me on the arm and said, 'It's okay, dear. He just doesn't want to eat anymore. It's time to stop.' And there it was, time to stop."

Food is what gives us life. It is the equivalent of sunlight to a plant. Fasting in many cultures is seen as a way of practicing dying. As our bodies begin to die, there is a clockwork as old as nature that ignites.

Some of the first organs to lose blood, to lose their batteries, are those of the digestive tract. Our brilliant biological systems know to reroute blood to the brain, lungs, kidneys, and liver; hunger and thirst begin to vanish. I know this information is graphic, but if we begin to accept the reality of our bodies and the bodies of our loved ones, we are more likely to be present, even in the hardest of times. One of the perennial pieces of wisdom shared by hospice nurses is to let our loved one know it is okay to leave us when it is time. Many deaths are prolonged by the sense that we need to stay alive for our family. Doing the impossibly difficult thing of letting a loved one know that you are going to be okay will reduce suffering. There is a time when we no longer need food.

If you were to design your own funeral or memorial, what would it look like?

Imagine if your grandmother decided that she wanted to make her own coffin—pick the wood, make the measurements, draw up a blueprint. Imagine she invited her bridge circle to join her, to saw, sand, primer, paint, and line it with her favorite plush material. What if she went further and made a themed coffin? Maybe she was in love with Elvis or wanted to be buried in a giant ladybug. What if she saw this as a brave and joyous way to face the inevitable, to take ownership of her own death and have some say in how she would be celebrated and remembered? What if she scripted her funeral, sent detailed instructions about who she wanted to speak and sing, and then shopped for and got the best deal on a cemetery plot or cremation service? Then let's say she negotiated a good price on a venue, designed the invitations, and made sure she knew who was writing her obituary.

At this point we can end this thought experiment because it isn't hypothetical; it is exactly what the Kiwi Coffin Club in New Zealand is up to, and they are growing in numbers by the day. In perhaps the most delightful end-of-life video ever made, they dance their way through a musical number, introducing their efforts to reclaim and make joyous the very fact that they are going to die, and sooner rather than later. They show off the "glory boxes" they designed themselves—from one that's Elvis themed to one covered in leprechauns and shamrocks.

"Face it," they sing, "a funeral's got to have soul."

About fifty or sixty people met as part of the initial club, but it's taken off. Now people are replicating the model throughout New Zealand and as far afield as Ireland. Part of the incentive is financial—a gold and mahogany casket can cost $5,000 (NZ), while you can order a wooden box through the Coffin Club for $200 (NZ). The grim reality is that the elderly are taken advantage of for all manner of services, but none so savagely as they are in matters of death and dying.

Part of the incentive for the Coffin Club, as their song—and the way they sing it!—attests, is personality. As original club founder Kate Williams told *National Geographic*, celebrating death is just as important as celebrating life. It only stands to reason that a person's memorial should only be as staid as they themselves were.

"We never knew how awesome death could be."

One of my favorite humans to talk to about death is Greg Lundgren, which is why he appears so often in this book. Greg is first and foremost an artist, and he has been creating the skeletal structure of the Seattle art world for the past twenty years. He has done more to establish northwestern artists than any curator or critic, and this effort of his has always been self-appointed. A creative mind hates a vacuum, and he has filled the role of unofficial mayor of the arts in a fashion only Tom Wolfe could capture. In between throwing self-funded internationally acclaimed biennials or launching massive unlicensed public installations, Greg's "real work" is a business called Lundgren Monuments. Unhappy with the state of memorialization, Greg decided to dedicate the majority of his craft as a sculptor and glass artist to the task of reimagining the headstone, monument, and urn. In short: it's art for the deceased. He often says how he meets his clients at a time when every other encounter they have is difficult. "They're spending their time talking to doctors, to cops, to funeral homes, but I play the role of the one conversation that isn't depressing—the one conversation that they're excited about. I bring joy. I allow them to consider beauty in a chapter in their life that is devoid of it."

In addition to designing, casting, sculpting, and installing headstones around the globe, Greg decided the world needed a death boutique. Imagine if Jonathan Adler opened a sleek storefront dedicated entirely to the creative celebration of departed loved ones. Now imagine the boutique featured custom-designed urns by celebrated architects, porcelain plates made from the ashes of a loved one, oil portraits that seem to be painted by Dutch masters—an entire artistic playground designed to rethink death.

By now you are beginning to see that Greg thinks expansively. Understanding that his life's mission is to re-infuse art into death, it occurred to him one day that he needed to be speaking to the kids, not just adults. He has since published several books about dying for children, one of which, *Death Is Like a Light*, I write more about on page 104. His first, *The Greenwood Cemetery*, is a story about an eccentric scientist who passes away. His nephew inherits his estate and finds all these crazy contraptions, including a robot named THEO 3000 that has been designed to memorialize the late scientist. His nephew dutifully places THEO 3000 at his gravesite. As word gets around, the kids in the neighborhood visit the robot. They play with it and delight in its antics. Then someone says, "My mother loved talking, let's build her a huge phone!" And another says, "And grand-dad loved golf and eating banana splits, let's make him something special, something that fits!" One after another the townspeople commission artists to design playful representational pieces of those they've lost. It changes this cemetery everyone was afraid of to a wonderland of enjoyment and remembrance.

"If you think about it, a sculpture park is basically a cemetery for millionaires," Greg says, with plaques acknowledging not who died and when but who donated the funds for what. "The only difference is that there are no bodies." He thinks we should regard cemeteries as sculpture parks for the middle class. It can be a beautiful way to honor someone and to protect sculpture. A meaningful piece does not need to be expensive.

Greg has himself delved into memorials as quirky as THEO 3000. After seeing the way a sculptor friend of his made likenesses of the bride and groom for the top of a wedding cake, Greg wondered if the same might be done effectively for someone who died. Why not make action-figure sculptures that memorialize a loved one? In miniature form they could be engaged in fishing, dancing, reading—whatever they loved to do in life. Greg now offers this as an option to his clients. But what resonates with him the most personally is portraiture. "I commissioned friends to make a portrait of my dad," he said. "I had these two paintings made, and they became two of the most precious possessions that I have. They evoke a lot of memory and emotion about how I see my father. One of those portraits lives in my dining room and I see it every morning when I eat breakfast. It feels like a healthy way to memorialize someone. Not like a cemetery that you see only every so often. Not like an urn that can be spooky. It becomes a family heirloom."

Briar Bates did not intend the water ballet to be a memorial. If her life had taken a different track, she would have been right there splashing around with all her friends.

Briar, an artist, was forty-two, dying of an aggressive cancer that had only been diagnosed months before. "When we found out she was dying," said her friend Bevin Keely, "I went over and asked what kinds of things were on her wish list. What was she hoping to get done in the next five years that we might cram into the next four months? And it was all about making the things in her sketchbooks come to life, to get that beauty out into the world."

The *Seattle Times* reported that as she lay in bed for hours, she looked up at a chandelier she'd made of Barbie dolls in swim caps, set in a classic Busby Berkeley–style formation. For someone like Briar, the inspiration was clear: a water ballet.

"The water ballet was meant to be an expression of joy and silliness," said Bevin, "something to brighten the world and add to its beauty. She said her artist's statement for the piece was to be HAPPY!"

"When Briar asked me to produce the piece," said Carey Christie, another friend of Briar's, "I did not feel as though I could possibly turn her down. It wasn't just because she was dying and I wanted to be of service. I also wanted to be near her because suddenly there was a scarcity of hours I could ever spend with Briar."

Briar gave instructions about everything from what fabric the costumes should be made from to the formations and movements she wanted to see. She gave detailed notes to the creative and dedicated souls who helped her execute on her vision. The ballet would be titled "Ankle Deep" and, she said, would be performed in the large concrete wading pool—a favorite for children—at Volunteer Park in Seattle.

A few weeks after Briar died her friends gathered to dress and put makeup on for the event. Then they headed for the park. On cue the fifty dancers dropped their caftans, trench coats, and coverups, revealing textured green swim caps and floral-patterned suits or swim trunks. They splashed around in formations in the pool to songs like Bobby Darin's "Beyond the Sea" and "Happy" by Pharrell Williams. A little girl dancer was lifted into the air. A bubble machine filled the air for the finale, and confused but merry bystanders got into the water themselves.

The performance was creative, quirky and joyous, and full of friends loving and leaning on each other. "That water ballet was a way for us all to do something life affirming in the face of our collective loss," said Bevin, "to remember what we love about each other and, in particular, our friend Briar, and to share that love with everyone else."

"Anyone could do this kind of project," said Carey. "And I hope more people do it, because life is this incredible gift, and death helps us recognize this. We need more than a place to put our grief. We need opportunities to express our overwhelming joy at being alive, and we need to do it together."

Holly didn't ever want to talk about the fact that she was dying. She and her husband pushed notions of it away. Even as friends gathered by Holly's bedside, they were told not to discuss it, not to let Holly know she was in hospice.

It was stressful. Her friend Andrea wanted to talk and cry together, but because there were two dramatically different narratives going on, she couldn't. Every conversation she had with Holly in the last year or so of her life stayed on a surface level, whereas once the two of them had been so close.

But after Holly died, Andrea said, she got the opportunity to understand how Holly had reckoned with her death. Holly had been a longtime collector of stuffed animals—everyone knew this about her. Although she used some of them in her work as a therapist, she was childlike at heart; most of the stuffed animals were for her exclusively. She bought them whenever she traveled, and her husband always got one for her for her birthday.

In Holly's last weeks her mom was sitting with her, and Holly asked her to get out a piece of paper and write down all the stuffed animals' names. She wasn't naming them for the first time—they had long had their names, but Holly hadn't recorded them. By doing this, by sitting with her mom and making a registry of stuffed animals, Holly was saying two things: first, I'm going to die, and second, when I do, I want to be sure that someone knows these animals' names, that the names go with them.

After she died Holly's friends were invited to come to her apartment and mourn her together. And then they were invited to adopt a "fur baby," as Holly had called her stuffed animals.

Andrea adopted Riley, a cuddly raccoon with soulful eyes. She and Holly's other friends emailed Holly's mom with photos documenting the outcome of the adoption process, which creature they'd each ended up with. Seeing the critters in their new homes and with those who had loved Holly was comforting to her mom.

Like Holly, Andrea is a therapist, and she keeps Riley in her office. Though Andrea sees adults, not kids, she said they notice him immediately. "I explain to them, 'A friend died, and this was one of her fur babies, and his name is Riley. Do you want to hold him?' And some people do. He's very snuggable," Andrea said.

Memorials can be as formal as a glass urn, as tangible as an action figure, as symbolic as a free ice cream sundae, as gleeful as a bunch of grown-ups doing ballet in a wading pool, as comforting as a stuffed animal. And though we can't change the story of someone's death, from memorials we can derive great joy and maybe even create some good.

Is there an excess of medical intervention at the end of life?

When former Senate Majority Leader Bill Frist was a boy in the 1950s, he recalls, he would go on rounds with his father. "And by rounds," he said, "I mean bumping along country roads in his car. Pulling up to a house, doctor's bag in his hand, and entering a dark and gloomy room to sit bedside a woman who was seriously ill. I would watch him go to the edge of the bed and touch and hold the hand of his patient, while I sat near him and listened to those conversations. Talk about an introduction to the holistic, the social, and the spiritual of dying."

My good friend Dr. Ira Byock likes to remind us that "death is not a medical act." However, doctors and nurses straddle the frontline between life and death. For a minute think about what it might feel like to be an oncologist facing an afternoon in which you have to tell a thirty-year-old new mother that she only has six months to live. We turn to our doctors to tell us how long we have left, what pain we might feel at the end, what things we can do to extend our life, should we fight or surrender. In our war on dying, doctors play arbiter, judge, healer, general, emperor.

How did we get to a place where we have placed far too many roles and far too much pressure on one human?

Most people you talk to in the profession will tell you that our medical system, our care model is without question run by nurses, and this prompt speaks to their role too. Their list of duties runs deep: to be present to dying patients, nurture and comfort the families, perform procedure after procedure. This is all in an environment where emergencies happen minute by minute and hospital administrators pressure them to limit patient time and streamline everything they do into line items. To be a nurse is to be simultaneously an Excel sheet, a patient saint, and an endurance athlete. If our medical system is in fact broken, we need to consider how you physically break something? Something breaks when its dynamic ability to bear pressure fails, causing it to collapse. I would argue that we need to ask less of our medical professionals, not more. Death is not a medical act—it is a community act, a human act, and it requires that we all step up and bear the weight.

A doctor in Greenville, South Carolina, told Angel Grant and her family that her dad's cancer would kill him within a year. Angel felt his words were hollow, uncaring, unaware. Filled with grief and her guilt for having not spoken to her dad in a year because of a family conflict where sides were taken, she lashed out. "I let the doctor know that while this may be a habitual conversation for him, it was not for us. I informed him that his casual lack of emotion or empathy was carrying the message that my father is dying. My stepmom's husband. My uncle's brother. My grandmother's SON. Is DYING. Then I stood there, teary and burning, holding primal, aggressive eye contact.

"I watched him soften in a way I was unprepared for," Angel said. "Nothing stared back at me through his eyes except compassion. And he said, 'I'm sorry if I communicated this in a way that didn't feel human. You're right—I do have to have these conversations way too frequently. But I want you to know that I became an oncologist because I was once standing where you are. My dad died of cancer, and I felt like there was nothing I could do about it.'"

"I've witnessed grief so aggressive," wrote ER doctor Jay Baruch, "that I feared for my safety. The adult daughter of a patient once charged at me, ready to hit me, only to collapse at my feet. Another time an adult child grabbed my white coat, pulled me out of my chair, and, refusing to accept what I was saying, demanded that I leave the family room and do more for his now-dead parent. I've also sat before dull nods, as if the family had been awaiting this heartbreak but didn't know when it would appear."[1]

⁓

Neil Orford is a doctor and the director of intensive and critical care services at a hospital in Australia. When he came to his first death dinner he had plenty to share about his professional experiences. After all, over the past twenty years he has had thousands of conversations with patients and their families about dying. He knows what it looks like when a family is grappling with complicated medical information and healthcare systems—and with overpowering grief. He knows what it looks like from a personal point of view too, but he hadn't shared much about the latter until the death dinner. In fact, when he came to the dinner, he didn't expect to share about his father at all.

When his father was dying, Neil explained in a personal piece he wrote for an Australian newspaper, he didn't feel his father's doctors listened to him. When the family expressed their fears that Neil's dad would be kept alive only to die at the hospital soon after, the doctors and nurses would only talk about resuscitation. The doctors would not be available to talk about treatment limitations until the next day, or the day after that. The palliative care referral did not come for a week. "I had imagined I would be able to smooth the bumps for my father and my family. I was wrong, and there are lessons I've learned."

"At his most vulnerable," Neil recalled, "my father suffered, and we were treated clumsily. Over ten days in the hospital he became progressively more distressed and frightened, and lost strength and dignity. When he developed urinary retention and couldn't empty his bladder, it took more than 24 hours for a catheter to be inserted, despite his extreme distress. When we asked if he could have nighttime sedation for his delirium and agitation, we were told he couldn't because of his brain injury. Yet at night we were called and asked to reassure and comfort him while urgent sedation was organized."[2]

Ultimately Neil identified himself to his dad's care team as a doctor himself—something he'd been reluctant to do—and was taken more seriously in his advocacy. The family got quick and effective palliative care, and his father died peacefully. But Neil felt it came at a cost. "A cost to my father, who suffered when he could have been peaceful. A cost to my family, left to feel guilty for demanding comfort over cure. A cost to me, because the days spent advocating as a doctor could have been spent grieving and saying goodbye as a son."

The default, according to Neil, is set at intervene. Dr. Ashleigh Witt, who works in an emergency department, agrees. "Palliation is hard for many doctors because we like to fix things," she wrote. "We like cures. We're excellent at saving lives, but struggle to accept we can't save everyone. And a good death is as important as a successful resuscitation."

She must intervene if the family requests it, even when she knows it will only cause trauma. "If a person's heart stops, we can perform CPR. CPR requires me to put my weight onto your elderly parent's sternum and push. To do this effectively, I will inevitably break some of her ribs. This sounds horrible, but if we don't do that, the heart doesn't pump blood to the body and without blood, we die." Whereas a young heart is likely to restart, the same is not true for the elderly. "When I am the medical registrar at a code blue [when someone is experiencing cardiopulmonary arrest and requires resuscitation] that involves doing CPR on an elderly person," Ashleigh explained, "I usually go home after work and cry. We're causing so much trauma to a frail person's chest, when realistically every doctor in the room knows the outcome will be death—regardless of whether we do CPR for ten minutes, one hour, or three hours. The patient's ribs are cracked and their final moments are traumatic. They are surrounded by doctors, not their children. That's not a 'good' or dignified death."[3]

In this impossible situation many remarkable doctors and nurses thread a needle between compassion and procedure. And many in the system get it right—or as right as is humanly possible.

"When we are afforded the proper time," Neil writes, "we are patient, we listen, explain, repeat, and eventually move together through the dying process. We don't rush; we get to know each other, trust each other, and over hours, days, weeks, move from focusing on the disease, to focusing on the person."

Molly Jackson, an associate professor at the University of Washington School of Medicine,[4] vividly remembers how she was taught to do this, to be with the dying, during her third year in medical school. Her teaching physician said, "I'm going to give you this patient, who is dying of AIDS, and it's going to be an amazing experience, to walk alongside him at the end of his life." Molly was ready, eager to sit with the patient's family and talk about symptom management. She was surprised, then, when the physician started out by addressing the patient's mom—the patient couldn't communicate at this point—with an open-ended, "Tell me about John."

"At that point," said Molly, "I understood what we were really there to do. We were beyond saving John's life, and now we were going to help John's mom with his death. I realized that a big part of what we're trying to do at the end of life is to give those who remain a meaningful or positive memory of the dying experience and have their loved one truly known by the people who are caring for them."

Molly acknowledges that she was very fortunate to have been assigned to the compassionate doctor she learned from, and that medical schools still have work to do to make sure this is the experience of every student. Out of 122 medical schools in the United States, only 8 have mandatory coursework in end-of-life care[5] And even though, as I wrote in Chapter 1, there's a billing code now for having difficult end-of-life conversations, it hasn't measurably changed the extent to which doctors have them or the extent to which patients hear them.[6] The reasons for this are complicated.

"Doctors don't know *how* to talk about it," said Dr. Tony Back, a leader in the field of palliative care. "They know it's important, but they don't know what to say or do." That's why he started Vital Talk, a nonprofit focused on increasing the communication ability of doctors and nurses. "Our inability as a medical community to talk about this hamstrings us. People talk to strangers about dying more than they talk to their doctors. Thirty percent of people who are dying of cancer have their first conversation about dying with a stranger. Then, at the very last minute, they're saying things to their doctor out of emotion and desperation and fear. They say 'do everything,' but what they don't realize is that they're going to end up on a ventilator, and they can't be in a place that can be a closure place for them."

"It gets really complicated in the nitty gritty of the decision making," said Molly. "We're improving our partnerships with patients and trying to help them understand the reality of what medical interventions will look like at the end of life, but it's hard to do. There are a lot of interventions that I worry are more likely to result in prolonging life but adding to suffering—and I share that openly with patients and their families—but it is hard for them to imagine what that really looks like. I feel it is a failure of our profession when our work prolongs suffering that leads to death—that is, prolongs a poor quality of life with no hope for meaningful recovery."

You need to understand that so much of this is new—for doctors and nurses as well as for patients. Molly went to medical school in the early 2000s and said that many of her teachers and mentors were paternalistic in their approach to death care. Her father, who is also a doctor and went to medical school in the 1970s, certainly didn't have formal training in talking about death with patients. But he also didn't have as many treatment options for his patients. It used to be that when people got diseases, they often died from them. Now there are so many choices, so many layers to navigate, and we're all learning how to do it together. Molly now helps teach patient-doctor communication and professionalism to medical students and is encouraged by how her millennial students have responded to this topic. "Their style is team oriented, patient oriented, and spending their time on efforts that are valuable for both individual patients and society— they're interested in justice and equality."

The pressure to figure out this balancing act is more imperative by the day as the costs of medical care soar. A single dose of a newly approved leukemia treatment is $475,000. How many days of life would you pay half a million dollars for? And how does that differ based on age and quality of life of the patient? This is horrific math to consider.

"It may be a different conversation when you're talking about a seventy-two-year-old versus a thirty-two-year-old," Molly said.

"And we can't say what's the best or what is the worst for any human. We have to let them define that."

There are so many components far outside of a doctor or nurse's hands—and even out of the patient's. Remember, Angel's anger at her father's doctor was spurred by her guilt over fighting with her dad. There can be cultural complications too, such as when an elderly Korean patient defers to his son's decisions, as is Korean custom, and the son sees his primary purpose as doing everything possible to honor his father. Decisions about medical intervention thus get tangled up in the messiness of human relationships.

Although there are necessarily no easy answers, there is a light that filters through this seeming chaos and pain, and that is presence.

Tony Back is a Buddhist and has spent years working with his teacher, Roshi Joan Halifax, exploring every angle of his training as a doctor, realizing that he has been taught to project a shield of invincibility and impenetrability. "Not a recipe for success, my teacher would say. She keeps reminding me to drop my shield, to try to live this way: *strong back, soft front*. Rather than giving in to what's expedient, to live with principles. Instead of leading with invincibility, to enter with attunement. It takes some training— at first I just felt exposed."

But attunement happened through practice. He gravitated toward Zen Buddhism because of his work in palliative care and has been a Zen practitioner for fifteen years. "I didn't know what presence was," he said. "In medical school they teach you it's a magical, charismatic thing. But it's not a matter of charisma; it's a matter of practice. If you can't be with yourself and all your own worries and fears, there's no way you have the ability, the presence to be with your patients."

Tony talks about the value of silence. Of knowing how to cultivate an ability to be silent within yourself so that you can give a patient the space to show up. Cultivating a quality of silence or a quality of presence is not limited to Zen practice; all faiths include contemplative practice, and the arena of mindfulness and meditation is an open route for anyone who is curious.

There are powerful tools to help healthcare professionals tap into that presence, like Schwartz Rounds and Death Rounds, which encourage healthcare professionals to come together in an open forum to discuss their feelings around mortality. Anchored on the calendar regularly, the Schwartz Rounds begin with a panel discussion of an interdisciplinary group, ranging from chaplains to social workers to physicians. The panel gives a brief presentation on a case or a topic, and then caregivers in attendance are able to share their views or feelings about it. Death Rounds are monthly discussions wherein caregivers are invited to talk about what it's like to care for the dying and what, if anything, they are struggling with. According to a study of Death Rounds, 76 percent of participants felt they were worthwhile and should be incorporated into ICU rotations.[7] An evaluation of Schwartz Rounds showed that caregivers who took part were better able to be compassionate and responsive to patients and their families, better team members, and had lowered feelings of stress and isolation.[8] Although all of this is encouraging, it's also very difficult to put into practice. Again, healthcare workers are being asked to do more with less.

If you look at the medicalization of death for long enough, it begins to feel like a Kafka novel—no time for providers to be reflective because of tightened budgets; tightened budgets because we're intervening more and more to little result; we're intervening more and more to little result because providers and patients lack the time to be reflective about it all.

Knowing what they know, seeing what they see, do doctors and nurses die differently from the rest of us? Dr. Ken Murray wrote an article several years ago called "How Doctors Die" that went viral. In the article he suggested that the doctors he knew did not want the same treatments they gave to others. Palliative care advocate Ira Byock has reported similar anecdotal experiences. "The terminally ill colleagues I've known, including those I've been privileged to care for, have usually been willing to use medical treatments aplenty as long as life was worth living, and took great pains to avoid medicalizing their waning days." But the research studies on the subject—though very new—suggest the differences in end-of-life treatments between doctors and nondoctors are slight. Why might that be? "Perhaps like nearly everyone else," Ira posited, "when life is fleeting, physicians find it difficult to follow their previous wishes to avoid aggressive life-prolonging treatments."[9]

What I take away from all of this is that it is one thing to believe something with your logical mind, with the support of statistics or medicine behind you, and quite another to be facing down decisions about your end-of-life care. We have this desire for doctors to die vastly differently from how we do. We want therapists to be very good at talking to their families about hard issues. We want comedians to be funny, even on a bad day.

Stu Farber found himself in the crosshairs of this human dilemma. He founded and directed the palliative care service at the University of Washington Medical School. He developed a palliative care training center so that young doctors could be better prepared. And then he was diagnosed with terminal leukemia. Tragically, his wife was diagnosed with the same illness soon after. Stu was at once doctor, patient, caregiver, and teacher. Even with all his knowledge and preparation, his wife said that knowing when to say "enough" about his own care was difficult.

She told the *Tacoma News Tribune,* "I sat with him at the [hospital] bedside, and I said to him: 'You know, if Stu Farber were sitting here right now with this family, he would tell us it was time to go home. And he sat up and he looked at me, and he said: 'Yes.'"

Do you have your will, advance-care directives, and power of attorney complete, and if not, why?

My mom gets a hard shake in Chapter 1, where I pinned our family's inability to talk about death and illness on her, and yet it should be noted that she is also the principal inspiration for my work. One night we were driving home from a piano concert, and out of the blue she began to talk about what she wanted to have happen when she died. She let me know that her house was designed so that a nurse could move in to her second floor and take care of her when she met that chapter. She didn't want her life to substantively change; she was averse to the idea of a nursing home and wanted to end her life in her little house perched above the Willamette River. She didn't want my brother and me to be burdened with the detailed care. She reminded me that she wanted to be cremated and let me know that it was already paid for and where the service was to be performed.

I mumbled some affirmatives, at a complete loss for words, and she continued. All her paperwork was in two places. The things we would need immediately were in her file cabinet under "In Case of Emergency" and included doctors, prescriptions, medical records, advance-care directives, a living will, and a DNR form. The safety deposit key was in the top drawer of her desk, and my brother and I were already authorized to access the vault. There we would find bank account numbers, info on her stocks, an updated and notarized will with specifics about her desired fate for each item in the house. There was also enough cash in case we had to make quick decisions and needed the money to do so.

I dropped her at home, thanked her for her thoughtfulness and candor, and drove off into the night, feeling two very distinct emotions. One was respect—for her courage and thoroughness. The other was lightness. I wasn't melancholy, but as she began to talk I'd felt an unbearable burden identify itself. The weight of her death, the potential of the grief, the number of decisions amidst the pain—all came crowding down on me while she was talking. Breathing in my face. And then with this magic trick of clear communication, she snapped her fingers and it was gone. The burden and weight I didn't even know I was carrying had vanished. She told me how to honor her, she told me what she wanted for her last months and her eventual death. This is among the greatest gifts my mom has ever given me.

⌒

Tyler's stepfather had a will, but he had not revisited it in fifteen years. He left everything to his wife, Tyler's mom. When Tyler's mom, Doree, died two years later, Tyler was the central beneficiary of their estate, responsible for sorting through their vast art collection. Doree was an artist, and Tyler had inherited her passion. When he and his stepbrothers divided up some of the less valuable artwork, it saddened him to see his stepbrothers summarily put them on eBay. Although he acknowledged it was their right, it magnified a divide—a tension that no doubt started because Tyler's role in the inheritance was greater than theirs.

Under the simplest of circumstances, resolving estate matters can get complicated, and it's more so when there are multiple marriages and stepsiblings to contend with, when there is little in the way of liquid assets but a whole lot of objects that mean different things to different people, when one child of the next generation inherits more than the others. All these things were in play for Tyler. Siblings—unclear about what their deceased parent wanted—often resort to the competition with one another that may have marked their youth.

One of his stepbrothers died before the estate was settled, and Tyler and his surviving stepbrother haven't spoken in six years. "We each needed time," he explained. Before their falling-out over the particulars of the estate, they had agreed that they would spread their parents' ashes—which had been purposefully mixed together—at a beach designated in Tyler's mother's will. Those ashes are sitting in Tyler's closet still. "I don't feel morally right about spreading them without my stepbrother," he explained. So he is waiting for the day when the two reconnect.

"When I die," Tyler's father—who is still living and in good health—says to him now, "Everything I leave you will fit in a shoebox." No rooms full of art, no items to sift through and catalogue. He was joking—and promising—that he'd keep it simple.

Many things ran through Chanel Reynolds's mind while she sat in the ICU. Her husband was just forty-three. They had not anticipated that either of them would be here, in a waiting room, while the other lost a grip on life. She thought—no, lamented—to herself: *I don't have my shit together.* Among the many stressors Chanel faced on ultimately losing her husband after a cycling accident was how she would manage financially. They had not signed their wills. She didn't have important financial or insurance information or even crucial account names and passwords to all their bank accounts.

According to a 2011 survey, 57 percent of US adults don't have a will. And that's not just twenty-year-olds we're talking about. (More on that demographic later.) A shocking 44 percent of forty-five- to sixty-four-year-olds haven't signed a will.

Chanel vividly remembers sitting with lawyers and financial planners in the weeks and months after her husband died. "I was asking them questions about probate," she said, "and how to consolidate our 401(k)s. And they stared across their desks at me and said, 'You know, we don't have our wills done either.' I thought, 'Who's running this monkey show? What's wrong with all of us?'"

The simple legal truth is that if you die and don't have a will, then your estate goes into probate and the state has to figure it out. And the order of people in charge and who is in charge of what may not be what you'd want. As Chanel points out, "It might not be someone in your immediate family that you want to find private items, like sex toys. Or if you do have personal requests like wanting to get buried in your Elvis jumpsuit, please tell me and let me know where it is."

These are some of the less controversial scenarios, of course. But as Chanel recalls, "Things can get complicated really fast. That's one of the reasons why my situation struck me so hard. I'm a Caucasian, middle-class, college-educated, English-speaking project manager. If the world goes sideways on anyone, I was set up to handle it better than most, and it was still so hard I thought I almost wouldn't make it."

Chanel's experience inspired her to launch gyst.com (Get Your Shit Together), which walks users through important components like living wills and life insurance. Her story resonated with the broader public immediately, garnering the interest of agents and publishers, and she has a book, *The GYST Guide: How to Finally Get Your Shit Together (Because Hoping for the Best Is Not a Plan)*. Clearly, this subject—in the hands of a human being who has experienced it rather than the hands of a lecturing lawyer—has a gravitational pull. And yet most of us don't have a signed will. Where's the disconnect? Is it that the idea of a will and power of attorney are so unpleasant to think about? Is it that we see it as a chore, a daunting task to be completed, like our taxes—but with an unknowable deadline instead of a reliable mid-April "post-by" date?

Heather Harman is a twenty-two-year-old at Drury University, in Springfield, Missouri. A star basketball player just months away from graduation, Heather is at the beginning of her adult life and yet is only too happy to talk about death. In fact, she thinks more people her age need to talk about it. Although the minimum-wage retail job might not make *estate* planning a prerogative, advance-care directives are important at any age. At Children's Hospital in Seattle, for instance, young patients fill out living wills so that their care team knows what's important to them in the event they can't communicate it.

For Heather's senior project, she chose to look at why more college students don't have advance directives. She hosted four death dinners of different Drury populations, from student athletes, to Greek life, to freshmen, to dorm residents. What she found was surprising and also, well, not. Out of fifty participants, half said they were comfortable talking about death. That's better than expected. But only nine had actually ever had a conversation about death with their families. "How can you be comfortable talking about death," Heather marveled, "if you've never talked about it with your family?"

Heather teamed up with a professional facilitator, who began each meal by asking the participants to picture their best day. People answered that they'd be with their family or with friends, and they didn't have a looming deadline. Then the facilitator asked, "If you're in a situation where you're in a bad car accident or become terminally ill, and the likelihood of you having that good day again are slim, would you change your end-of-life wishes?" There was no wrong answer, she emphasized.

"It was hard for them," Heather said. "Many people said, 'I just don't want to think about it.' They really try to separate themselves from their own death, in a way. . . . Many of them associated advance planning with having a negative outlook on life. They said, 'I'm too young. I'm way too young to be thinking about death.'"

A common refrain from the sixty-and-over crowd is, "I just don't want to be a burden to anyone if I'm sick." And yet Heather's participants expressed the same sentiment. "'Burden' was the word that came up over and over again," she said. "Not just an emotional burden, but a financial burden. It was more important to them that their families not be burdened than that their own wishes were honored." The average age of Heather's participants was 19.66 and straddled the line between what we've come to think of as the "entitled" millennials generation and the more financially conscious Generation Z. And yet for both, money mattered.

Heather found the hardest discussions were the ones with the freshmen. She felt they were reserved, maybe even afraid. She didn't leave the meal thinking they'd gotten much out of it, but she was pleasantly surprised. "All said in a survey after that they would be somewhat likely or likely to initiate a conversation about death after the dinner."

And to nudge them in the right direction, Heather has plans. She made a younger teammate on the basketball team dress up for Halloween as the Grim Reaper and pass out advance directives

all over campus. Next she's planning a party with campus nota-
ries as the special guests.

Heather is clearly a remarkable exception. As we discovered,
most Americans, young and old, are not prepared for end of life,
sudden or slow. Why don't we all have our paperwork neatly
filed, waiting in case of an emergency? It seems like it would
fit nicely in an application for life insurance or a step your primary care doctor or health insurance provider makes sure you
complete. Perhaps we include advance-care directives and health
proxy documents with every marriage license or when you sign
an employment contract.

Or maybe what we need to do is get a community energized
around advance planning—to initiate a marketing push for taking
greater responsibility. In LaCrosse, Wisconsin, a town of fifty-
two thousand, 95 percent of the residents have completed an
advance care directive. Their remarkable effort over twenty years
has reduced end-of-life expenses in LaCrosse to 30 percent below the US average. You don't have to be an economist to grasp
the savings available to us at a national level. LaCrosse decided
to face the stark reality that end of life is inevitable and made a
community-wide effort to both talk about death and plan for it.

And yet, here is the irony: it wasn't until I had completed five
years of dinners and started writing this chapter that I personally
completed my own paperwork.

What is the most significant end-of-life experience of which you've been a part?

Death has the quality of a diamond. It is irrefutable and prismatic; with every angle you turn, it emits new light and new perspectives. Telling the story of deaths we've witnessed helps us to examine new perspectives and identify our own wishes. These stories are our way of coming to know ourselves as we weigh our sensibilities against the protagonist's. Without sharing these stories, we deny our ability to become fully expressed. This is why we read literature and why myths are important.

Laurie Anderson was with her fellow musician, best friend, and husband, the legendary Lou Reed, when he died of liver cancer. He pursued all options in his treatment and did not give up until the last half-hour of his life, when Laurie wrote that he accepted it "all at once and completely." She wrote in a moving piece for *Rolling Stone* how he asked to go outside their home, into the morning light. He knew what was happening. "I have never seen an expression as full of wonder as Lou's as he died," she wrote. "His hands were doing the water-flowing 21-form of tai chi. His eyes were wide open. I was holding in my arms the person I loved the most in the world, and talking to him as he died. His heart stopped. He wasn't afraid. I had gotten to walk with him to the end of the world. Life—so beautiful, painful and dazzling—does not get better than that. And death? I believe that the purpose of death is the release of love."[1]

Lisa was in her early seventies when she was diagnosed with ovarian cancer. Her primary instinct then, as it had long been, was protecting her children. Her son had just had his first baby, and her daughter was then pregnant with *her* first. It was a rich and beautiful time in their lives, and Lisa did not want her medical issues to distract from that. It took a while for Lisa to reveal to her children the extent of her illness. It only became clear to her daughter, Jamaica, months later—by which time Jamaica's baby daughter was nine months old—while Lisa was visiting Jamaica at her new home and plainly very sick.

"I remember sitting outside on our porch with her and asking her if she wanted to come stay with us," said Jamaica. "And my mom said, 'I don't want to die in your house.'" It was the first time they had spoken about what was going to happen so directly. Jamaica asked her: Why not? Why not die in her house? "My mom said, 'This is your new house, and you're getting established. I don't want that to happen here.'" Jamaica felt differently about it—she didn't want her mom anywhere else. Lisa's son felt the same way—he wanted his mom close. But Lisa remained insistent about not being a burden.

Lisa and Jamaica's dad looked into renting apartments nearby, but before they could commit to anything, Lisa's health took a turn for the worst. A late-night trip to the ER was followed by a hospital admission a few days later. Then a personable doctor Lisa took a liking to, who Jamaica described as a bit of a hippie but with the look of Austin Powers, spoke frankly with Lisa about her plans during one of his daily check-ins. When he asked if she would continue staying with her daughter after her hospital stay and Lisa explained her reluctance, this doctor turned to Lisa and implored her with a knowing shake of his head, "Don't deny your children the opportunity to care for you."

This was powerful advice, a different perspective from someone she'd come to trust, and something in Lisa's approach shifted. She suddenly stopped resisting being cared for as much. She was willing to ask things of her son and daughter. She recognized that it made sense not to push her children away when they were trying to give her love and wanted to care for her.

During Lisa's last weeks Jamaica was deeply involved in her physical care. "I remember talking with my dad and brother and them saying, 'It could be months or a year . . . ,' but I think a daughter with a mother is different—you're intimately involved in the care aspects. You see and touch it and start to live it. Being with her every single day, she couldn't escape what was happening to her body, and neither could I. And that was okay. I think it was therapeutic. It's heartbreaking, but when you put your hands on it, when you see from one week to the next how hard it is and you see the daily changes taking place, it makes it real and makes it tangible. There's hoping for the best, and then there's a point of acceptance. I felt a bit at peace when that point of acceptance happened. When my dad and brother were still asking, 'How will we prolong her life?' I was reading the situation very differently."

Years before, Jamaica had worked in the Peace Corps in Africa, and Lisa had spent time with her there. As they talked with Lisa's Austin-Powers–doppelgänger doctor about their memories of Africa—a place he'd also worked as a doctor for Médecins Sans Frontières (Doctors Without Borders)—he sighed nostalgically. "They sure know how to die there," he said. Jamaica knew this to be true. When someone was dying where she'd lived in Guinea, you knew it because *everyone* gathered. "Family and friends would come and everyone would just sit for a half day, or a full day, outside the home and come in the home to visit whoever was sick and support the family," Jamaica remembered.

Lisa wanted this too. As she became ensconced in Jamaica's home, the front door was never locked and rarely even closed.

Family and friends came in and out to visit, and during the final weeks of Lisa's life the house was a hive of activity. Lisa's brother and sister-in-law came from a thousand miles away and set up camp. Lisa's sister-in-law cooked huge meals, and nightly dinners in Jamaica's backyard included anywhere from six to fifteen people and usually no fewer than two children. "It was one of the worst periods of my life and one of the best," Jamaica said. There was always someone there to pitch in and do what needed to be done. And Jamaica never opened the refrigerator without seeing it stocked with food people had dropped by, a gesture that meant so much to her both practically and symbolically. "My mom's parting gift was bringing all of this together. It was three weeks of family. Three weeks of a party. There was lots of wine and lots of good food, and she was in the middle of it all. Even the last night, when she wasn't conscious, she was in the sunroom but we opened the windows so she could be looking out at the table outside."

After Lisa died, Jamaica recognized that she had left another gift to her children. Because she'd had time to prepare, Lisa handled as many of the logistics of her passing as she could, from insurance matters to going through her jewelry, and assigning who would get what. Though Jamaica acknowledged that still many logistics fell to her dad, she appreciated that she had the space to just grieve. "I can see how heavy the burden of administration is for many people, and there wasn't any of that. If you want to make the comparison with Guinea, there are no forms to sign there after someone dies," Jamaica said. "There are clear steps and traditions, and there's a good reason for that—it means that you don't need to make decisions. You can go through the motions of what tradition dictates and focus on your grief."

Jamaica works as a demographer, so issues of birth and death have a very different context for her professionally. In her work she looks at death numerically—she has to. But living alongside her mom as she died gave her more of a sense of immediacy, of how she would handle her own death. She got everything in order from her life insurance to her will. "We're all going to die," she said thoughtfully. "We can either accept it or make it a shit-show for everyone around us."

Jamaica thinks that Lisa's attention to the details also helped her to let go at the end. "She said 'I've had a good life. I lived really well. I'm really lucky.' That's how I want to feel. You can always say there's more to do—and there is. Or you can say it's been a pretty good run and now I get to just be at peace."

～

It was a hot night in August, balmy and fragrant in Boise. Several of the state's most influential business leaders came striding through the front door: the CEOs of Albertson's, Norco, St. Matthew's Hospital, Blue Cross Blue Shield. The rambling house filled with laughter and warm hugs as the guests arrived. It seemed that everyone in Boise had played at least eighteen holes of golf together within the past week alone.

There was no difficulty for this group to drop into real talk. Any notion that Idaho folks are buttoned up or had a midwestern fear of hard conversations was immediately dispelled. These people came to talk about real shit.

That night, because the group was mostly in their fifties and sixties, I knew which prompt would resonate. I began: "What is the most significant end-of-life experience of which you've been a part?"

The conversation immediately centered on taking care of dying parents. The death of a parent brings us to a cocktail of emotions, that mixture of regret, bitterness, intimacy, and the potential for great healing that are the hallmarks of our relationship to the people who gave birth to us. I have heard dozens of stories about what it is like to take care of a parent in their final chapter. How stressful and confusing it can be and how caregivers have even felt at points that they resent and despise those they are caring for.

People are surprised to hear others express the same sentiment. They had felt they were alone in what they labeled a shameful lack of generosity and are gratified to learn it's common. It reminds me a bit of postpartum mothers who don't feel they can say out loud that they're sad or that they don't like motherhood or that they don't feel immediately attached to their infant. When we avoid expressing what we sense is shameful, those feelings do not cease to be true—in fact, they tend to ferment and grow. On this night in Boise we broached all of this and more.

Amanda Fisher is a partner in an investment firm. Amanda had faced a quandary several years earlier when her mother's health took a profound turn for the worse and she had quickly been admitted into hospice in southern Texas. Amanda had gotten the call from her uncle; she and her mother hadn't spoken in years.

She faltered a little in her story at this point. She squeezed her husband's hand and told her group of colleagues stories about her upbringing that she'd previously kept to herself. Amanda's mother had her when she was sixteen, and, as Amanda plainly put it, "she was a junkie." At that the table set a new course. In four words Amanda pushed us out into deeper, wilder, more unknown waters. We would not be talking in platitudes and generalities tonight. We would speak simple, raw truth.

Amanda told us briefly about her childhood. Her mother came and went, stealing her away from her grandmother's stable home in the middle of the night with a new boyfriend, only for her grandmother to rescue her from dangerous situation after situation, eventually becoming her legal guardian. Things hadn't improved in her relationship with her mother over the past thirty years, but when Amanda heard she was slipping in and out of consciousness three thousand miles away, a voice inside of her was clear: go to her. She told her boss in the private equity firm where she worked that she needed to head to her mother's side. She would be gone for a few days, possibly a week.

A week became two and then three, stretching into a month. Her mother's health rebounded when Amanda arrived, and mother and daughter entered a dimension of their relationship that neither had access to before, as if some secret door appeared in a house they thought they knew well. Amanda ultimately lost her job at the firm while she provided round-the-clock care. But Amanda considers that month one of the most important experiences of her life. They found closure; old wounds surfaced and were cleaned and bandaged. She was able to watch her mother slip with grace into the next world. Tears streamed down Amanda's face as she spoke about her mother's final moments, about how sacred it felt to hold her hand as the woman who gave her life took her last breath.

Two years later Amanda's beloved grandmother's health dramatically turned for the worse. Amanda was now on a fast track to partner at her firm. She dropped everything, boarded a flight to Chicago, and spent the next three days in the ICU. The terror of losing her grandmother was palpable in her retelling. Amanda's grandmother had saved her, raised her, loved her, and taught her how to be the kind of woman who could forgive and take care of her estranged mother. Amanda's grandmother was the stable ground Amanda stood on and the person to whom she owed the most in the world.

Amanda sat and held her grandmother's hand for hours. The doctors felt Amanda's grandmother's condition—though critical—wasn't likely to change over the next few days. Amanda weighed her options. Work was piling up, and Amanda had not forgotten how she had lost her private equity job when she'd spent too much time away caring for her mother. She felt a sense of urgency about finalizing a deal she was working on in Boise and decided to take a quick flight home and then return to her grandmother's side within forty-eight hours. It was a hard decision, but Amanda felt she had to show strength and follow-through at work. When she landed, her phone was afire with messages. Her grandmother had lost consciousness and died.

Amanda had to pause in her story. It was if she was trying to regain her breath. She began to talk about regret, the sharpened knife of a feeling that digs somewhere in between heart, lung, and bone. "There is nothing I wouldn't give," she told us, saying each word slowly, "to go back to that moment and make a different choice. . . . Not the job, the house, our boat, none of it. I wasn't there when she left this world. . . . I made the wrong decision."

Gail Ross is a literary agent who is always working—not in a workaholic way, exactly, but rather in a way that clients become family, and the books she works on shape her view of the world as much as her view of the world shapes her books. Books are a calling.

Gail's work also brought her closer to her widowed mother, who had an apartment in New York City, the epicenter of the publishing world. When Gail traveled there from Washington, DC, for meetings, she'd stay with her mom—so for two or three nights a month for thirty years the two had time alone together. They went out to quiet, comfortable dinners and then returned to watch *NCIS* or *Law and Order*, her mom's favorites. Without the mother-daughter angst that had defined their dynamic when Gail was growing up, they became close.

As it happened, one of Gail's subject-matter specialties was death. She had worked on books about palliative care, near-death experiences, and grief and healing. So when her mother was diagnosed with terminal cancer, Gail knew the territory they were entering well. "I was surrounded by people who were writing about death, who were living a life where death was made normal," she said. "I had become obsessed with questions surrounding death: How can it be less mystifying and scary? How can it be part of one's spiritual journey?"

"It doesn't mean I'm completely at peace with my own fears about death," she clarified. "But because of this work, I'm not afraid of being around someone who's dying."

As the end came closer, Gail moved in with her mom in New York. "I went there with the idea that I'd do some work, I'd go to some meetings, and I'd be able to take care of my mom too." But things went downhill fast, and none of that came to be. "This sounds really crazy, but other than when my kids were newborns, this was the only time in my life when I was completely focused on something else. I wasn't thinking about work; I wasn't thinking about the world. It was just about caring for my mom." It was exhausting physically and mentally, and though Gail knew more than the average person about hospice, she came to realize that it did not mean she would have access to helping hands and open arms all the time. The truth was that the hospice group was very busy. It was December, the holidays were at hand, and though the hospice team was kind, they weren't around much. Gail's mother also didn't like having nurses in and out all the time. The result was that Gail and her sister cared for their mom around the clock until the last couple of days, when a night nurse came to let them get some sleep. Gail even slept in a bed with her mom during part of the last week. "I remember she woke me up one night and told me about the beautiful, medieval church she was in. Then another night she said she was so mad at me for making her leave home and live in a hospice facility. I said, 'No, Mom, you're here. You're in your apartment.' To which she said,"—Gail laughed recalling the moment—"'Well, the help here is terrible.'"

On the last day the nurse woke Gail and her sister up at 4 A.M. and said it could be any minute. For the next twelve hours Gail and her sister took turns going to sit with their mom and finally turned on a movie in the living room and went in to check on her every five minutes. "Then we walked in and she just seemed different. It seemed like she was taking her last breaths. To be sure I put my hand on her neck to feel for her pulse. After a second or so and with me and my sister standing there, our mom took her last breath. It was intense. But it was beautiful."

Most of the stories I've shared in this chapter are about caring for a dying parent. When I use this prompt at dinners, most of the stories shared are indeed about caring for parents, as that is the caregiving situation we are most likely to experience.

I haven't myself cared for a dying parent. I was too young when my father died, and he was living in a facility away from our home. But I was surprised how even *thinking* about caring for my mom carried a rich opportunity for healing in our relationship.

My mom and I haven't been close since I was a toddler. As early I can remember, our relationship was one of distance. Our lack of connection is not a judgment; raising me and my brother while my father was suffering from dementia and then full-blown Alzheimer's was a living nightmare for my mom. Plus, she didn't really have the mothering gene to begin with, and her upbringing in a single-parent family in Ogden, Utah, in the middle of the Depression didn't help matters. Nor did leaving the Mormon Church and her family at eighteen. It was as if life had only become a thing of beauty for her when she met my father, and within ten years of finding her twin flame, his mind began eating itself. My family's story is one of getting something beautiful and then having it taken away. Until recently I have been unconsciously recreating this traumatic loop.

The physical dis-ease between my mom and me grew when my father died. Then the combined forces of adolescence and menopause made things downright toxic. She kicked me out when I was fifteen, and after returning for a year, I moved out for good when I was seventeen. We have always put on a good show at family gatherings and public affairs. My mom is an elegant, charming, intelligent, and beautiful woman, and we both know how to work a room. Below the surface, too, there has always certainly been love. But there has also been a great deal of anger, blame, and pain.

Occasionally in life we have revelations. They don't come on any kind of schedule, and when they are authentic, they change the shape of your life. Some people call it a moment of mental clarity, some consider it divine transmission. It doesn't really matter what terms we use; powerful revelation is a component of being human. I was attending a meditation retreat when I received a revelation about my mom. In an instant I went from trying to quell my busy thoughts to gaining complete clarity about her death and her final months. Not in a psychic way and not about her contracting any kind of illness, but about me and my role during the end of her life. It came to me clearly that I was going to be the one who was there for her when she inevitably began her final months, weeks, days.

Nine months passed, and I didn't call her to tell her about my new insight. On a November Saturday in Los Angeles I found myself engaged in a writing assignment as part of a men's course. Our instructor asked us to think of all the women in our life who we had wronged in some way. Not focusing on what they did or didn't do to us, but just focusing on those to whom we had done something we regret. He wanted a prioritized list: mothers, wives, exes, daughters, friends, lovers. Times when we were mean, nasty, cold, aggressive, hateful. "Make a list," he said. "Get it all down." There was not a ponderous pause when the writing assignment began. Pens hit the paper, and the lists grew long.

After twenty minutes our instructor had us stop, and said, "So gentlemen, I wasn't completely honest with you. Those lists aren't just a writing assignment, what you have in front of you are *call lists* . . ."

I will let you feel the wave of sensation that hit that room.

"I want you to take the top five women on your list, go ahead and cross off anyone who is in jail or if you called them it would put you or someone you love at risk. However, the others are open game. Turn to the man next to you—you will be partners, and you will provide support for each other while you make the calls. You have one hour. Call these women and apologize. Be authentic. Decide in advance what you can honestly say that you are sorry for. They will be able to sense any bullshit immediately. Make the calls on the shorter side, let them know that you would welcome an opportunity to talk at length about this soon, but today you just wanted to acknowledge that you had done something you wanted to apologize for."

I immediately decided that calling either of the mothers of my children—yes, there are two different mothers—would complicate the ongoing struggle I had at the time around our parenting plans and custody. Glimmering at spot number three on my list was my mom. And below her a woman who I had been very cruel to on a date, and below her a brilliant colleague I had excommunicated for something that wasn't worth the punishment. The list got less interesting from there. In my life I have focused most of my poison on the principal relationships in my life, preferring an acute instrument of disrespect to a shotgun blast.

I called my mom, heart pounding, and experienced pure relief at the sound of her voicemail. My apology partner Matt dialed his mother. And in the middle of their longish, heartfelt chat, my phone buzzed: "MOM." I took a few steps back and answered.

We exchanged a couple of pleasantries, and then I started in. I shakily told my mom about what I'd realized about her final months, and that I was sorry I hadn't called her before to tell her. That despite the emotional distance between us, she could count on me to be by her side, every step of the way, however her final months and days took shape. That she could rely on me and not worry about who would be managing the details, that I would take care of her. Tears drenched both phones. I'm sure she was as surprised to hear this as I was to have the revelation. It had always been assumed that my brother would solely be there for my mom, shouldering the weight, as he always has taken that role.

Through her tears she acknowledged how difficult it must have been for me to tell her this and how profoundly she appreciated me. And then something I can only refer to as magical happened.

My mom apologized.

She took full ownership for the distance in our relationship and apologized for neglecting me as a child.

Since I was young my mom had always been on the defensive. Anything that felt like criticism from me, my brother, or anyone else was immediately deflected and often turned immediately on the detractor. Telling my mom I was going to be there for her as she died, in her most vulnerable physical state, instantly melted a forty-year dynamic between us. By facing death with my mom, I was able to forgive her and to see her more clearly. Death became a way for us to come together.

For me, then, the great potential in this prompt is that just as it uncovers moments of beauty in caring for another human being at the end of life, it also invites us to think about the trials that may yet come and presents opportunities for healing before we're faced with that final chapter.

Why don't we talk about death?

In the hill towns of northwestern South Carolina, repressed conversations are as common as dogwood trees. Even though Becky's oncologist had made her situation clear as a bell, death and even cancer were topics that were not allowed in her family. Becky's father had even gone so far as to say, "We don't use the C word around here." Despite this—or perhaps because of it— Becky had signed up for a death dinner and death meditation, which was why she was headed through some of the worst traffic in the United States—that outside of Atlanta—to get to a little town called Serenbe.

Becky hastily found a place on the plush carpets at the eco-community and resort that oozed with southern charm. The death meditation was about to begin. Angel Grant, who conducted the session, spoke with confidence that filled the darkened room. Several dozen southerners shuffled into corpse pose, lying on their backs and closing their eyes.

"Notice how you respond internally to what I'm about to say," Angel said. "Just notice the sensations that occur in your body. There's no right or wrong way . . ."

"Of the over seven billion people who are on the earth right now, almost none will be alive in a hundred years . . ."

She paused, letting it settle into the room. "The state of mind at the time of death is important—if we're grasping for life or feel hindrance or resistance in any way, our suffering is exponentially greater. Some hospice nurses have shared that patients with unfinished emotional business suffer the greatest physical pain during the dying process.

"With an exhale, begin to soften muscles, from the crown of your head all the way down to the arches of your feet. Drop in to this room, the body, this breath . . . ."

As Angel led the group through a guided seventy-five-minute meditation, describing the dying process in intimate detail, Becky had a realization. "The way Angel guided the meditation, she made my body so personal to me," Becky said. "I had never thought that way. I'd never understood that my body is my ally. It was the first time I got in touch with everything my body has done for me. Understanding how, as we near death, the organs shut down, in sequence, and that they do it in a way that protects us. It felt divine to suddenly understand that. I hadn't gone anywhere near these ideas because this kind of thinking was off-limits. I wasn't able to even talk about the fact I was sick."

In Becky's experience her body had always been "not enough." It was a nuisance and had, at times, been a tool, but she'd never understood it as something to glean wisdom from or an entity to listen to. Her focus had been on *shutting down* messages from her body. With this new perspective still buzzing in her, the group slowly came back to life, and as she looked around the room she could see the glint of realization in everyone's eyes. In the next room the clatter of plates beckoned the group around small tables of eight. Candles were lit, wine was poured in deep glasses, and sumptuous dishes of southern farm cooking filled the tables.

Each person shared with their tablemates the name of a loved one who had passed, lighting a candle and raising a glass in their honor. Then Angel asked the first prompt of the evening: Why don't we talk about death? Are you afraid of it? What about it scares you?

"I'm not one to speak in front of people at all," Becky said, "but I went first, and when I opened up, it all came out. I had never been able to tell anyone those things, what I was facing. I was afraid to die because I knew that my family would go against every wish I had—where I wanted to be buried, how I wanted to be buried. And I felt like my cancer was taking up all the air in my family. Here I was, creating this turmoil for everyone. I felt like the purple elephant in the room. I felt like a reminder, like it wasn't my right to be sick. And instead, I was in this group of intelligent people who cared about what I had to say, and they listened and asked me question after question. When I started talking, my cancer was all of a sudden not so big."

This evening was the first crack of light in Becky's healing process. Being able to openly talk about death, a topic that occupied her mind since her cancer diagnosis, enabled her to identify a real fissure in her life. Becky decided not to pursue another round of chemo, much to the dismay of her family, and instead took a road trip across the United States to swim in the Pacific Ocean.

In the fall she decided to attend a retreat in Mexico with Canadian physician and author Gabor Maté. Every day Becky gathered in a circle captained by Gabor, and with no official agenda the group descended into their repressed pain, fear, anger, and sadness. Gabor calls his process "compassionate inquiry" and likes to say, "the most compassionate thing I can offer you is honesty." Put in a more scientific context, dozens of studies have proven that repressed emotion and repressive emotional models of behavior cause disease.[1] Gabor's methods are reminiscent of a healing ritual in a Zambian tribe that Michael Meade talks about. In this tribe, when a member of the tribe gets sick, they believe an ancestor's tooth has lodged itself in the person. The tooth will come out, they feel, as the truth comes out. So they come together as a tribe, and the sick person reveals whatever intense emotions they're experiencing, and so does everyone else. The tooth comes out, and everyone is cleansed, when these painful truths are given a voice.

And so it was that Becky shared with this group of strangers something that few people knew: that she had been sexually abused as a child and what it felt like when her parents negated the story. The rape denial was one of the many ways that Becky learned not to ask for what she needed or to talk about the hard stuff. Now, with stage 4 cancer, she was playing by different rules. She was willing to talk about it all.

For three nights of the retreat the attendees also gathered for a ceremony that involves drinking a bitter brew that combined two jungle plants known in the West as Ayahuasca. The shaman who oversaw the ceremonies approached Becky at the end of the retreat and asked if she wanted to spend the next three months on a very limited diet—no salt, shellfish, sugar, pork, fermented foods, dairy, citrus, or strong spices like garlic, onion, peppers— and come back to complete another round of Ayahuasca in February. The shaman felt that if she did these things, by the end of February the cancer would be gone. Becky had all the doubts that are probably rising up in your mind: How could the cancer be gone? Had she stepped into some mind-control cult? How foolish was she to think that doing some drugs in a jungle and talking about her feelings could have an effect on her dying body?

When you're staring down a bullet, you will try some wild things. Becky went all in and spent the next ninety days in a state of relative exhaustion, struggling to maintain this vastly new diet. As she neared her return to the jungle, her desire for sugar had started to vanish, and she had begun to see the foods she ate as a direct energy source, as medicine, not just something to fill her up. When Becky saw her oncologist after her second trip to the jungle, he reread her scans and bloodwork several times, mystified. Becky's cancer was in remission. The survival rate for stage 4 ovarian cancer is 10 percent.

The takeaway is not that everyone should run to the jungle and drink a strange concoction with Peruvian shamans. I have no idea what caused Becky's healing or how long it will persist.

However, she is a different person from who she was when she first drove to the Chattahoochee Hills to talk about death for the first time. She has the confidence to know that her experience and her emotional pain need to be shared instead of stuffed away—and the radiance that issues from her is contagious. She has regained the energy of her youth and has changed the way she thinks about herself and her future.

The message to shout from the mountaintop is not that the bad stuff that happened to you in childhood is going to kill you; instead, it's this: if you do talk about it, your chances of healing are much higher.

The work of Nobel Prize–winning psychologists Daniel Kahneman and Amos Tversky shed powerful light on why we *don't* talk, and from them we can learn why we continue to avoid topics like death, why Becky's family won't allow the C word, why 100 percent of us aren't organ donors, and why we don't all have living wills, health proxies assigned, DNRs filed, and a cemetery plot paid for and waiting for us.

Our avoidance of the death talk seems to be nestled inside a systemic error in the way we think. Newsflash: we don't make rational decisions. Our leading economists and behavioral scientists long assumed that we do and so wondered why their predictions for what people would buy and how they would act were so wrong.[2]

Kahneman and Tversky set off to understand where we misjudged reality, where our own computing systems were making consistent systemwide errors. What came to light through their groundbreaking research was that humans operate with a vast network of biases and heuristics, or patterns of thinking that have lodged themselves in our operating systems as we've evolved. As Kahneman wrote in his seminal book *Thinking, Fast and Slow*, "we can be blind to the obvious, and we are also blind to our blindness."

Many of the invisible biases that we operate under each day come to bear on the question of our mortality. I think this inquiry deserves an entirely separate book, but bear with me as we poke our head into the rabbit hole.

Let's start with one bias that influences how we do or don't talk about death: base-rate bias, also known as base-rate neglect. It is the tendency in humans to neglect the generic data that pertains to *us* in favor of data that relates to only a specific case. The base-rate data for all humans is that we are going to die. There is a 100 percent mortality rate, has always been, arguably will always be. Yet we don't *feel* like we are going to die. We are here, breathing, thinking, reading—that counts as data too. And so we neglect the irritating reality that we are mortal.

Let's add on another bias, the normalcy bias, which is the tendency to believe that because something hasn't happened to us before, it is unlikely to happen. We can underscore this with the affectionate term YOLO, or "you only live once." As far as we can remember we have only been born once, and most of us have no memory of a death. And so it is almost impossible to take death into consideration.

Because we are now fully in a bias dance, let's weave in the courtesy bias, the tendency to give an opinion that is more socially correct than one's true opinion so as to avoid offending anyone. This particular bias is a silent killer, and it reduces the likelihood of us bringing up death with a parent or spouse to a mere probabilistic sliver. The courtesy bias is also alive and well in doctors and nurses, as they give patients a much rosier outlook than what patients are actually facing. As mentioned earlier, in a study of thirty-five hundred people, only 16 percent of metastatic cancer patients reported an accurate prognosis estimate.[3] Our mortality catch-22 is summed up in a tidy package by Kahneman: "When faced with a difficult question, we often answer an easier one instead, usually without noticing the substitution."[4]

The good news is that even though we are likely to be blind to what is right in front of us, our brains are not built out of stone; they are flexible, alive, and constantly changing. Because of neuroplasticity, new pathways in the brain can be opened up every day.[5] There is an old Native American parable of two wolves that captures, through storytelling wisdom, what it took science a while to catch onto:

A grandfather is talking with his grandson and he says there are two wolves inside of us which are always at war with each other. One of them is a good wolf, which represents things like kindness, bravery, and love. The other is a bad wolf, which represents things like greed, hatred, and fear.

The grandson stops and thinks about it for a second, then he looks up at his grandfather and says, "Grandfather, which one wins?"

The grandfather quietly replies, "The one you feed."

How do you talk to kids about death?

Many people can't remember when they first realized they were going to die and describe it less as an "aha!" moment and more as a growing understanding, the way the existence of a tooth fairy is slowly explored and questioned, leading then to bigger questions about Santa Claus, magic, and heaven.

But some people do remember this moment clearly. Jenna can't remember how old she was, but she distinctly recalls she was with her family on vacation, driving over the bridge from Coronado, California, to San Diego. She remembers thinking, I'm *me*. And one day I will stop being me. Nancy said, "I remember being about four or five and freaked out by the idea of infinity. I just remember looking at my feet on the bathroom floor and suddenly realizing the world would go on and on without me in it 'until infinity.' Around the same time, I would always ask my parents if I would die before the morning, so I must have been a little obsessed about this."

Steve said he was about ten, playing Nerfball in his basement. As he absentmindedly played with the ball, a glimmer of understanding took hold and then settled in. He panicked and ran to talk to his mom about it. She was seemingly prepared. She calmly brought him up to her room and took out her Bible. She read to him and explained how there was a room waiting for him in God's house. It was nice to hear, he said, but did little to staunch his childhood existential crisis.

Karen was older, around eleven or twelve, and her death awareness was triggered when the bus she and her friends were taking to camp flipped over on the roadway. Although no one was seriously injured, the trauma of the event—of her parents rushing to get her and bring her home, the sight of the bus turned on its side—made its impression. As her parents tucked her in that night, she verbalized what had been slowly dawning on her: "I could have *died* today."

Angel was five, and she was playing in her room alone. "I remember all of these pieces falling in order, falling together, so that I just sat there beside my bed thinking silently, 'I'm gonna die. Everyone's gonna die.' I remember looking at my body and thinking, 'This just ends.' I was scared and confused, thinking about all the adults in my life who walked around acting like this wasn't the most important thing. I wanted to say, 'What are you doing? Don't you realize you're going to die? That we all are?!'" Angel took her newfound realization to the adults close to her, who all said some version of, "Oh, don't worry about dying. Just don't think about it."

Angel has thought about it every day since.

Every other weekend Angel would spend Saturday night with her dad and stepmom in their small South Carolina town, and they'd go to the Southern Baptist church the next morning. Angel vividly remembers the preacher saying, "If you don't get saved, you're gonna burn in hell when you die!" Angel had already been baptized by a different church. But the imagery the preacher used scared her enough that she wanted to be sure she had her bases covered. So she was baptized by the preacher's church too. Then during another week's sermon the preacher said, "If you've been saved and you don't feel any different from how you did before you got saved, you're gonna burn in hell!"

Angel considered the question: Had something changed in her from before her baptism to after? Did she feel different? Not really, no. She panicked. Getting saved must not have worked on her this time either. Each night at bedtime she imagined what it would be like to burn in hell.

She never talked to her dad or stepmom about her fears. She'd play Monopoly or Scrabble with them on Saturday night, then she'd go to bed and think about church the next morning. Then she started getting violently ill every Saturday night, to the point where her parents took her to the ER on numerous occasions. At first no one could figure out what was going on, but they finally determined she had an ulcer. One ER doctor spoke to her kindly and said, "Honey, is there something you've been worried about?" But she said no—she simply didn't have the tools or understanding to recognize that her fears of burning in hell had made her sick. It wasn't until much later, when she was in college, that she understood.

As I think about Angel's story, I gravitate not so much toward the fear of hell—though there's certainly plenty to unpack on that front—but rather to the notion that this five-year-old was grappling with big concepts of life and death and existence without an adult to whom she could direct questions and have an honest and safe conversation. When we think about our earliest ideas about our deaths, who was there to guide us through the scary parts?

When kids ask us questions, we want to have the answers and worry it will just freak them out more if we don't. And yet there are a lot of things about death we *can't* have the answer to.

Katrina Spade, the founder of Recompose, which converts human remains into soil, has taken an environmental approach to talking about death with her kids. When they were two and five, she remembers giving them a bath and explaining the cycle of life. "First there's a chicken," she said, "and it eats the grass in our yard. One day it lays an egg. You kids eat the egg in your pancakes, and we put the eggshells in the compost to make more soil to grow more grass for the chicken. It's a cycle! And someday, when we die, we can put *ourselves* in the earth so that our own bodies will help grow grass, and who knows, maybe someday they will help feed a chicken too. And my work, as you know, is about trying to make that cycle happen a little more directly. Life and death are real connected, you know? When someone dies, the whole process starts anew."

Katrina was careful to leave room for her kids to feel the sadness too. She talked about how her son cried extensively after getting what looked like just a minor scrape. When she asked him what he was so upset about, he said, "Every time I bleed, it reminds me I'm going to die."

"Oh, okay," Katrina acknowledged. "You go ahead and cry then."

For her part, Angel doesn't know what kind of conversation she would have *wanted* to have at five. But she has two young nieces, and when they engaged her in a conversation about death, she answered in a metaphysical way. "I said, 'You know how our bodies seem so solid? If a strong enough microscope existed, you could see that our bodies are actually made up of tiny vibrating particles. Everything in the entire universe is. That energy, how the particles vibrate, doesn't have a beginning or end. If something doesn't have an end, that means it never dies. And if we're all made up of that, our bodies may die, but we don't, and we—all of our particles—are always connected, forever and ever.'"

Whereas Angel felt some level of grounding was important to offer her nieces, Greg Lundgren offers another perspective. He teaches kids to relax into the uncertainty, making it okay that there are no answers, that there doesn't necessarily need to be solid ground. He wrote a beautiful children's book on the subject called *Death Is Like a Light*. "I was renovating a work space I have," he said, describing his inspiration for the book, "and I noticed that a halogen spotlight was dying. It started to slowly flicker and then it would go out for a few seconds, and finally it died and the light went black. I thought, 'That looks a lot like death. There's no denying it, there's no fixing it.'" It led him to a whole series of maybes, connecting death to objects and experiences kids could understand:

"Maybe death is like school, filled with learning and friends, and you aren't quite sure where you'll go when it ends."

"Maybe death is like a milkshake with whipped cream, two cherries, and fudge, and when we reach the bottom, we can't hold a grudge!"

"Maybe death is like a ruler that only goes to ten. Just because it stops counting doesn't mean everything ends."

"Maybe death is like a flower—a daisy or clover that returns to earth when springtime is over."

Anastasia Higginbotham has also written a book for children on the subject. *Death Is Stupid* follows a little boy coping with the death of his grandma. He's not having any of the empty platitudes from adults, like, "She's in a better place" or "She can rest." Instead, he asks, "Would I be in a better place if I died?" and "Why can't she rest here with me and still be alive?"

Anastasia doesn't claim to have all the answers about how to talk to kids about death, and she doesn't claim to kids—even her own—that she knows what happens when we die. But she is clear on three things: first, you can help make what's scary less so; second, you can approach their questions with curiosity and collaboration; and third, you can watch them carefully to see how they're handling it.

The truth is that we often shut down kids' questions when they become too uncomfortable—for us or, we fear, for them. For instance, when six-year-old Polly asked her mom if their aunt Kay had been buried yet, her mom said no, she'd been cremated.

"What's cremated?" Polly asked.

"Oh, it's when a body becomes ashes and you scatter them around places that were meaningful to the person who died."

"So how does a body go from being a body to being ashes?"

This is where her mom got stuck. But going back to Anastasia's rules of thumb, she answered, "With fire. But it doesn't hurt at all. Still, honestly, I don't know much about it. Would you like to explore more about how it works?"

If a child moves on, Anastasia said, let them. If they come back to it, let them. And don't shy away from honesty about how the conversation makes you feel. "Allow yourself to say, 'I don't love to think about it,'" Anastasia said. "They might say, 'I don't love to think about it either.'"

One of Anastasia's kids was terrified of death, starting when he was about six. Each bedtime for a few years she would go to him to help calm his anxiety. "Sometimes I would say, 'You're thinking a lot about death, but we're very much alive right now. And no one we know who is close to us is sick, so tell me more about what that fear is about.'" Her son explained to her that he feared being in a situation where he couldn't move or talk but was still thinking. "I started to see those questions as a portal into how to learn more about my child," Anastasia said. "Where is he going with this? And how will it inform my own understanding—not only of my kid but also of what death might be like?" Their bedtime conversations led into the subject of what constitutes spirit. "I was relying on books I'd read and then adding to that my own belief that I do think there's a sort of *whoom!*, then off we go. I don't think that we get trapped." But as abstract as their conversations became, Anastasia was always, always careful to end by bringing her son back to the present and emphasizing reality. "I would say, 'You are in this bed, very much alive. I'm sitting next to you, very much alive. The trees outside are alive. No one is in danger here in this space. Let's feel your heartbeat in your body. Feel my hand touching yours.' It was a way to lead myself back as well. And I wasn't lying to him or saying, 'Don't worry about that,' but I was trying to bring him back to the now."

As comfortable as Anastasia is writing about death and talking about it with her kids, she was hit with a moment when she reckoned with just how forbidden a subject it is. She was at a bookstore in Brooklyn, preparing to do a reading of *Death Is Stupid* for seven or eight kids. She'd given them paper, glue sticks, and pictures of animals so they could make collages while she was reading to them. And then it hit her. "I thought, 'I'm about to open this book and tell them they're all going to die. What was I thinking? How did I think this was okay?'"

"I got to the page where it says, 'Eventually every life comes to an end.' And I just said the words and I took a deep breath and looked them in the eye. And let it be quiet. One girl looked at me with her bright eyes and nodded and gave me a half-smile."

Anastasia realized that she wasn't doing any harm by saying it, even if she had deep-seated cultural programming that told her otherwise. She understood that the conversation was going to happen to them anyway at some point, and here she'd written a book to help the discussion go gently. She kept reading.

Although approaches with kids will necessarily vary, the fact is that they're generally good at talking about death. It's only when they grow up and begin to see it as a forbidden topic that they shut down. By the time someone is in their fifties or sixties the chances that you're going to affect their views about death are minimal—those views are pretty set. But children can grow up looking at death differently—not as a topic to be avoided but one to ponder with curiosity. That's why I encourage inviting kids into conversations about death. If they don't want to talk about it, fine. But if they gravitate toward it, let them in.

Do you believe in an afterlife?

It was the middle of night, but I woke up for some reason I couldn't grasp. I was thirteen years old. I looked at the alarm clock on my bedside table, taking note of the time: 3:43 A.M. Guessing that I had to pee, I headed down the hall to the bathroom. But no, that wasn't what had woken me up. I walked back toward my room, stopping to look over the railing. It was a big house, too big for our small family—just my mom, brother, and me now. From that vantage point you could see the living room, kitchen, and dining room. Everything was silent. Too silent.

I went back to my room and went back to sleep. When I woke in the morning the silence was still there, but unlike the night before, I immediately knew the message it held. That my father had died. I got up, walked down the hall to my brother Brian's room and found my mom and Brian holding each other and sobbing. The medical records confirmed that my father's heart stopped beating the night before at 3:43 A.M. He died in an assisted-care facility, twenty miles from our house.

I'm a hard sleeper. I have always fallen asleep easily and slept like a stone through the night. I don't profess to know what this experience was about or why it happened. I don't know if I believe in ghosts, and I don't have a strong conviction about what is on the other side of death. You would think that the afterlife would come up at most death dinners, but it doesn't, and on the rare occasions when it does, people don't seem to push their feelings and faith on others. Death is a land that has no experts— we are all looking into the void together.

I often encounter stories about near-death experiences and even more frequently hear the mysterious stories about a connection between those who are living and those who have passed. We could call these ghost stories, but that wouldn't do them justice.

There may well be a connection between our life and whatever afterlife exists; we just don't happen to know what it is.

In *Letters to a Young Poet* Rainer Marie Rilke reflected on the importance of not getting too entangled in fighting what we don't know. It is often quoted because it resonates for so many:

> Don't search for the answers, which could not be given to you now, because you would not be able to live them. And the point is to live everything. Live the questions now. Perhaps then, someday far in the future, you will gradually, without even noticing it, live your way into the answer.

Angel lost her dear friend Newa Hashim when he was shot and killed by a police officer in February of 1998. "Nothing I turned toward for relief alleviated the feeling that something terrible happened and justice was not there to meet it," Angel said. "It wasn't the most digestible companion for the persistent ache of loss."

Colossal redwood trees stood outside Angel's bedroom window, and she would look toward them for companionship. "On the rare occasion that the sun sneaked through the Arcata fog, it gleamed through the trees into my window. During those moments I started to sense Newa's presence in a way I didn't understand, but nevertheless, I would sit on the floor and let myself feel washed in it.

"I didn't spend much time thinking about whether I 'believed' he and I could actually contact one another, mostly because thinking about it prevented me from feeling him." What she did do was sit in deep, silent stillness for hours, receptive.

"At times," she said, "I would hear him somewhere inside myself quietly speaking to me or catch visual glimpses of him in a way that's hard to name. I never felt sure—or cared much—if my mind was manufacturing these experiences as a way to deal with the loss or if an actual unexplainable connection was happening.

"After many months of seeking him out in the presence of those redwood trees," she continued, "I had a dream one night where I got to spend time with him. In part of the dream he was rollerblading backward with a huge smile on his face in the sun. Moving farther and farther away from me in the sun, he said, 'Angel, you gotta let me go—you're holding me to the earth.'

"All at once I felt that he was okay, that it was all okay, and that I couldn't keep pulling on him to soothe my pain when I missed him terribly. I cried so hard in the dream, from loving him and from letting him go, that I woke up sobbing but resolved."

A few weeks later Angel's best friend, Becky, who lived across the country in South Carolina, went to a craft fair in Atlanta. At one booth she looked through the bracelets on offer and thought she'd get one to send Angel. She struck up a conversation with the jewelry maker, Cynthia. As so often happens with southerners, their friendly chit-chat quickly turned into deeply personal conversation. Cynthia told her of her son who had been shot by a police officer, how hard it had been for her to live without peace around it. Then Cynthia told her about a dream she'd had a few weeks prior. Her son had come to her in this dream—they had talked for a long time, and at the end he looked at her with love and said, "Mama, I'm all right. But you've gotta let me go. You're holding me to the earth."

Becky was the only person Angel had shared her dream with. She looked at Cynthia in awe and said, "Is your son's name Newa?" Cynthia started crying, shaking her head yes.

When Angel tells this story, which isn't often, she's sometimes met with looks of awe and sometimes looks of doubt. She shrugs the latter off.

~

Carine McCandless had a similar experience with her brother Chris. Chris's story was famously told in Jon Krakauer's bestselling book *Into the Wild*: as a young man, Chris walked away from his family and even his name and wandered the country as Alexander Supertramp. His sights set on Alaska, he entered the Denali wilderness underprepared for the harsh elements. After a series of missteps, he died 113 days later. For twenty years after Krakauer's book was published, the public did not know the full story, and many presumed Chris was selfish and irresponsible. In reality Chris and Carine's upbringing was abusive and filled with deceit, and his quest was not driven by a death wish but rather an attempt to heal himself. Although Carine knew this better than anyone, she did not set the record straight out of a sense of duty to her parents and a hope that they would learn from such a tragic loss and stop their deceit. The story is complicated, but as the years went on, Carine felt more and more troubled by how Chris's legacy was incomplete. Chris had been looking for truth at the end of his life, and Carine felt she was complicit in obstructing that truth. As she worked with Sean Penn on a film version of *Into the Wild*, it was an important step toward telling the rest of the story. But she was horribly conflicted, as she still had a relationship with her parents at that time. As Carine explains in her follow-up memoir, *The Wild Truth*, she sat in her living room one night, looking over the movie script and feeling totally bereft, at a complete loss. She started to cry, and though she felt silly doing so, she called out to Chris. "Chris, please! I just can't do this alone. Please, I need to know that you are here with me."

The next morning she was folding laundry when she got a call from a friend, Tracy, who she hadn't spoken to in years. Tracy apologized for the random call, but said she felt she had to reach out about a dream she'd had the night before. In the dream Chris had come to her and said, "Do you know who I am?" Tracy said, "Yes, you're Carine's brother." And then Chris told her "I need you to do me a favor. I need you to call her and tell her I am there with her." Carine was stunned silent, and as Tracy apologized for fear of upsetting her, Carine assured her friend that she'd bestowed a miraculous gift. "It gave me an incredible sense of peace and what I needed to keep moving forward," she said.

⌒

Roughly a year ago Monica's twenty-three-year-old niece, Megan, died tragically in a car accident. Since childhood Megan had had a way with horses. "Gifted doesn't speak to it, really," said Monica. "She had an uncanny way with horses that cannot be taught." At the time of her death Megan was living in Colorado and worked as the head wrangler on a working bison and cattle ranch. Soon after she'd arrived she struck up a special relationship with a wild mustang named Gus, who previously wouldn't allow anyone to ride him. This almost miraculous connection happened. "The two of them were like a machine that worked together," said Monica. "Megan trained Gus, and Gus trained Megan."

After Megan's death her devastated family went to Colorado for a memorial ride to scatter Megan's ashes. It was decided that one horse would be rider-less, and of course it was Gus. Gus had always been a bit of a loner, but during the ride he stayed particularly close to one rider. "He always kept Teya in sight," Monica said. Teya was Megan's only sister and her closest friend. The two always referred to one another as their "person."

At a designated spot on the ride the contingent stopped, and Megan's father, Ted, pulled out the ashes from his saddlebag. "Right as he did so," Monica said, "Gus laid down. He didn't just go down; he laid all the way down on his side, his head stretched out, his eyes open. It was the quintessential picture of absolute heartbreak." What was even more surprising, Monica explained, was that she had been told that Gus never laid down unless to sleep, let alone in the middle of forty other standing horses.

Tears streamed down the faces of the ranch hands as they watched Gus. They understood. Gus stayed down until the last family member finished spreading the ashes.

As the group rode back to the ranch, Teya and her horse separated themselves from the crowd. When the mourners regrouped at the corral, they saw a rider and two horses galloping toward them over the plains. As they came into view, it became clear that it was Teya, her head down in concentration, riding at full speed. And the horse riding alongside Teya was Gus—in full stride, in total synchronicity. Teya and Megan shared the same strong, full-bodied riding style, and both horses were running in the exact same full-bore, galloping stride. Monica said, "Those watching from the corral knew without any doubt that Megan was riding Gus and that she was riding with Teya one last time.

"I've always thought life is like a penny," Monica said, reflecting on the experience. "You can see one side or the other, but you can't see both at the same time. This side is life, and death is the other side of that coin. But it's all one thing."

Monica's musings about life being like a penny are amplified when we talk to people who *have* glimpsed both sides—people like Maya Lockwood, whose encounter with death was as close as anyone can go without going all the way over. And as many people who have had a near-death experience (NDE) will also attest, Maya considers it a great gift.

She was nine months shy of her fortieth birthday, living alone in San Francisco, when she got what she thought was a virus. She stayed home and rested for a few days, then went to work for a meeting, then felt sick again. This cycle lasted about eight days. She wasn't feeling great on July 2 and wanted to rest up so she'd be ready to celebrate on the Fourth with friends. So she texted them that she was going to lay low to try to get better. No one heard from her for two days. On July 4 two close friends went to check on her. They found her unconscious in the middle of the floor in her apartment, naked. She had urinated all over the floor and had green bile coming from her mouth. Her body was hot to the touch.

Maya's friends called 9 1 1, an ambulance came, and Maya spent the next several days in a coma as doctors tried to get to the bottom of what had happened. They speculated that it was sepsis or meningitis. (Ultimately the cause of her illness is still inconclusive, but Maya suspects sepsis.)

After four days Maya woke up, confused and disoriented. Though she'd been unconscious, Maya vividly remembers how pixilated the world was around her. And most vividly she remembers what it felt like when she surrendered. "I thought, okay, I guess I'm going to die. At that point the physical pain of the resistance and the battle and holding on to everything that I knew ended. There was no more pain. So then I became aware of this knowing that we're just a part of love . . . part of a love energy."

She told me it's hard to describe in words. Then she sighed and said, "It's wonderful."

When Maya returned to her job and her life, she was different. Outwardly it wasn't too obvious. She didn't get a face tattoo or spend all her savings on a Tesla. But unlike before, she didn't spend time on unnecessary drama. She could set boundaries, which had always been difficult for her. She became protective of her time to relax and rest. "People who have known me their whole life will try to get me involved in some drama, and now I will often say no. I never knew that hard *no* would create so much joy and happiness in my life.

"I feel like I had an operating system or computer that had completely crashed," she said, "and I was given a whole new operating system. Whatever viruses, processes I had struggled with in the past, like having strong personal boundaries or fear or worries or depression—they were gone. I had all this space in my mind to start creating and start learning."

Maya reports what many people do who have had NDEs: they come back from it unafraid to die. "I feel like we're given this chance to enjoy this realm in a physical form," she said. "We get a body with five senses to experience life. And it can be filled with joy and it can be filled with so much love and it can be easy. I'm able to now be in my forties and enter this new chapter in life with an incredible feeling of peace in my heart and my mind. It was an incredible gift. The near-death experience—knowing that death is nothing to fear—allows me to truly love and not get bogged down in a lot of dumb stuff."

The two major takeaways from Maya's experience, she says, are joy and love. "I got a second chance, and I feel joyful. It's not that I'm running around dancing. It's a quiet, content joy." She said she would love to share that feeling of not being afraid of death. "But I also think, 'maybe I'm not the person to share it, maybe it's not my job.'" She sighs again. "It's like a diamond. The most precious diamond. It's incredible."

It is interesting to think about the classic near-death experience narrative of walking into a world of light—light and flashes of light are consistent with ideas of the afterlife and the moment after death across cultures. New microscopic monitoring of sperm fertilizing eggs show that when an egg is successfully fertilized a flash of light is produced.[1] The spark results from the release of billions of zinc atoms, flashing at the moment of conception. The brighter the spark, generally speaking, the healthier the embryo.

No one can definitively say what to make of NDEs or the variety of ghost stories I've presented here. And again, I don't think that's the point. The point is that when we encounter these moments, if we turn toward them in all their weirdness, it allows for a sense of wonder. And I don't think the quest is to find the answer about death; it is much more important that our lives begin to follow the arc of an answer. I think Kyoko Mori said it best: "Everything we say about death is actually about life."

Would you ever consider doctor-assisted suicide?

Allie Hoffman is the person many celebrities and would-be celebrities call when they want to break some hard-to-swallow news to the mainstream. She runs the digital presence for Caitlyn Jenner's foundation and helped bring Alicia Keyes into the conversation about ending mass incarceration. Allie was fresh from orchestrating supermodel Geena Rocera's shocking announcement on the TED stage that she had been born a boy when she got a call about Brittany Maynard. Though Brittany was not (yet) a celebrity, she had the hardest-to-break news of all.

The general public had not heard the name Brittany Maynard. She was a twenty-nine-year-old newlywed diagnosed with a very aggressive brain tumor who wanted to legally end her life and make it easier for others to do the same. Doctor-assisted suicide, which we more frequently now call death with dignity, is not front-page news. It's *too* hot an item for personal narratives to be told. If you think the battle lines are drawn over abortion, imagine the passionate disagreements over ending adult lives. It is still such a taboo that even the discussion of it is suppressed.

Allie flew to Beaverton, a Portland suburb, to meet Brittany. "Brit was very logical," said Allie. "I noticed her mom and husband encouraging her to see new doctors and get new opinions. But she was rational. She wasn't emotive in the way you would perhaps expect. She had assessed her options and thought, 'This is going to be an awful death. My body is going to try to keep me alive while my brain kills me.'" Or, as Allie—who is never one to mince words—put it, Brittany understood that "hope is a motherfucker."

Brittany and her family had been living in California when she received her fatal diagnosis, but at that time California did not allow patients to end their own lives. So Brittany's husband, mother, and stepfather all moved to Portland, where they had to spend precious time seeing doctors and establishing residency before Brittany would even be remotely eligible for death with dignity—not an easy task while the effects of the cancer were amplifying by the week.

According to Allie, Brittany was pissed off that hospice was the best California could offer her, and she had enough resolve that she wanted to spend the last months of her life telling her story, with the hope that she could move the needle for others in her position. They shot a video, wherein Brittany explained to an unseen audience what her diagnosis was, how she and her husband had been trying to start a family when she was diagnosed, how she felt about dying, how reassuring it was to have the medication that would end her life on hand, and how she planned to die in her bed with her family and friends around her. Not surprisingly, the morning news shows wouldn't touch it. This is where grit came in; the team knew about a *People* reporter who wanted to cover right-to-die. Quickly People.com agreed to launch the video and write a story. Within a day four million people had watched the video, and since then Brittany's story has reached hundreds of millions of people, and her lively, photogenic face famously captured the cover of *People* magazine.

They had kicked the hornet's nest. The media frenzy was now relentless. Having cameramen posted on your lawn is never a good experience, and it is even harder when they are covering your impending death.

Allie received all the letters and emails on Brittany's behalf and so had a front-row seat to the passions raging on both sides. Many letters were from people fighting to save Brittany's soul. Many others were from those who supported her choice and wanted to help. And then, Allie said, "We got a beautiful letter from a mom and daughter in Arizona. The mom had been diagnosed with cancer, and she had a protracted battle. They didn't know how to talk about what was going on. But Brittany's story, they said, gave them a language and an understanding."

On November 1, the day she had chosen to die, Brittany awoke to a house filled with family and close friends. They all took a hike together, and then Brittany took her prescription and died peacefully at home as she wanted to.

Within two years the laws in California changed to allow death with dignity, and the importance of Brittany's advocacy role in making that happen cannot be overstated. Bringing it full circle, Allie said she had a friend from college who had the same cancer Brittany did. She used Brittany's law to die at home—in California.

⌒

I want to be clear that, although I think Brittany was a remarkable human, I am not a death-with-dignity advocate, nor am I an opponent. I find some truth on both sides of the argument. What I know is that if we suppress this conversation, we don't have an opportunity to make educated decisions. Ira Byock is one of the most outspoken detractors of doctor-assisted suicide, but he is not a faith-based detractor. He is a nonreligious Jewish doctor who is in many ways the father of US palliative care. He sees the current hype around death with dignity as missing the point completely. What we are facing, according to Ira, is not a lack of options but rather a lack of quality care at the end of life.

Like Ira, I am hesitant about the gleeful euphemisms that surround doctor-assisted suicide. The languaging "death with dignity" and "right to die," as he points out, is brilliant marketing. Ira takes particular issue with the phrase "physician aid-in-dying" and points out that this has a very different meaning. As a palliative-care physician, that's what *he* does, he said. He treats his patients' symptoms and supports them through what they need at the end of their lives. But that's very different from euthanasia. "In more than thirty-five years of practice," he said, "I have never once had to kill a patient to alleviate the person's suffering."[1]

Even with safeguards in place, Ira fears, assisted suicide puts vulnerable people at risk. He also worries that condoning physician-assisted suicide sends the wrong message—that it makes more sense to invest in letting the medical system kill people than doing the work necessary to make end-of-life care more effective. He points to the Netherlands, where euthanasia has been available for years, as an example of what could happen in the United States. People there have requested euthanasia for nonlethal conditions like pain, tinnitus, and blindness.

"I believe that deliberately ending the lives of ill people represents a socially erosive response to basic human needs," Ira wrote in an op-ed for the *Los Angeles Times*. "If we can stay civil and (even relatively) calm, we can debate physician-assisted suicide while also substantially improving end-of-life care."

If someone came to Ira and said they wanted to end their life, Ira would first and foremost listen. He'd say, "Tell me more. What can we do to lessen your suffering?" He would tell the patient that he personally couldn't write a lethal prescription but that he wouldn't stand in the way if they wanted to find another physician who might.

There is much that Ira has in common with proponents of doctor-assisted suicide. He thinks we need to die better. He is compassionate and wants, above all, to reduce suffering. He thinks we need to have more honest conversations about death. But then the roads diverge, the commonalities split, and how to achieve those goals looks very different.

Tony Back, the founder of the Palliative Care Center of Excellence, didn't feel strongly one way or the other about the Death with Dignity law that passed in Washington State in 2008. But what he's seen on the ground since has surprised him. The people he's met who have chosen this option have focused not on their misery and pain but on living their lives. Like Brittany Maynard, they are trying to pave a way for people like them in the future. And, Tony said, they put even more of their limited energy into preparing the people they love for a life without them.

"A retired teacher with ovarian cancer wrote letters to her daughter and granddaughter that they could open on big events: the sweet sixteen, the prom, the anniversary, the granddaughter of her own," Tony said. "A soft-spoken human resources manager threw, uncharacteristically, a huge party, where he reveled in the pleasure of all his friends being in the same room. A retired professor said, 'I just look at every single day differently now. I'll be sad to leave, but . . . you know? It's been a hell of a run.'"

It's not that every one of the people who wants to use the death with dignity option is so gracious and calm. And it's not that people who choose to die of illness more naturally can't also share and experience these things. But, according to Back, something about the intentional act of death with dignity brings everything into sharper view.

"Their courage and frankness astounded me," said Tony. "Especially since, after my research interviews, I would go back to my oncology clinic, where patient after patient would look sideways when I asked if we could have a serious talk today about what to expect with their cancer.

"What I've concluded," Tony said, "is that there is something enlivening about facing one's own mortality and vulnerability."

People who want to hasten their death might be focused on autonomy and control as a primary objective. That's only natural: not feeling in control of your life is one of the most anxiety-producing experiences in the world.[2] And if that's true when the control is around traffic or a delayed flight, imagine what it would be like if it was about suffering. When you remove the stress that comes with a lack of autonomy, people are better able to enjoy their lives—and even to heal. Dr. Mary Ruwart wrote that when her sister Martie was dying painfully of gastrointestinal cancer, she obtained a promise from the infamous Dr. Kevorkian that he would help her end her life when she was ready. Just having that promise, Mary said, helped Martie eat again and actually keep the food down. "Her need for pain medication dropped off precipitously. The transformation bordered on the miraculous.

"We learned that this was not uncommon. Evidently the fear of dying in pain is so great that it impacts negatively on a person's health." When Martie relaxed, it gave her body its best chance to heal. And although she ultimately took Dr. Kevorkian up on his promise, the end of her life was one where she felt in control.[3]

To Tony, though, much of the beauty of death with dignity is less about the sense of control and more about how the people who choose this path are leaning in to death, how they're willing to face it head-on. What that means, he said, "is they get to say everything they want to say. The people they want to touch, they get the opportunity to touch. They get to say, 'Hey, I'm really dying, this is happening.' As a friend or family member, you don't hem and haw when someone who is exercising their right to die calls on you to visit."

The thing that didn't just surprise Tony but also *changed* him was watching these patients' families. "When confronted with honesty and vulnerability, these sons, daughters, fathers, mothers, and friends responded—to a person—with love, generativity, and creativity. Not Hallmark card stuff—I mean jaw-dropping, Pixar-level wow. They thought of everything, far outstripping my medical training, and pitched in with these patients to create moments of great beauty and legacy, right in the fragility of the situation."Tony remembered a son telling him how, now that he's over the hump of talking about his parent's end, he gets it. And a daughter explaining how she and her mother planned that she would scatter some of her mother's costume jewelry in the garden with mulch so that the daughter might dig up a piece later as a nice surprise.

Since then, Tony said, "I try to ask myself every day: Could I live more like that? Could I acknowledge the fragility of right now? Could I stay on the lookout for a flash of sapphire under the dying leaves?"

What song would you want played at your funeral?
Who would sing it?

Angel and I were eating a rushed breakfast before a morning meeting. We'd picked a little diner in West Seattle that happened to be half record store, half greasy spoon. David Bowie's song "Sound and Vision" played on the speakers overhead, and as I checked my Facebook feed, a post stopped me cold: "It is as if the brightest light in the universe has burnt out. We will miss you starman." I felt a resounding "no" echo through my entire body. David Bowie was dead. "Sound and Vision" was playing as a lament.

I had never before been affected by the death of a musician or actor. I'd never judged this response in people, but until January 10, 2016, I had no way of understanding it. I had no way of knowing that Bowie's death would impact me so powerfully. Tears streamed down my face. Angel was immediately alarmed and tender, and I felt like I might start bawling like a child. It is not even that I am the biggest Bowie fan, but in looking back on this experience and my sense of grief and loss around his death, I realize that his existence—his incredibly bold, unwavering commitment to expand our consciousness, to push at the edges of convention or flat-out break them—made me feel safe in this world. In countless ways Bowie had given me and so many of us permission to explore our own edges. A world without him felt immediately less.

Bowie shows us that music touches a part of us that isn't necessarily logical, that goes where words can't and instead lands in the realm of feeling—this is why music and grief are so entwined. It is hard to imagine a funeral or a memorial without music.

I consider "What song would you want played at your funeral? Who would sing it?" as an icebreaker prompt, a safe question. It's a question you can ask your parents, your spouse, or grandparents without tripping the full-scale alarm that you are asking them to consider their own mortality. We live during the era of the playlist, and so it can act as a conversation starter that engages in an unthreatening way. I use it when I've gathered a bunch of strangers to talk about death, and though there is usually laughter and some wistfulness in the answers, you might be surprised how quickly this question can move into the depths.

I'm always struck by the diversity of the responses: one person wants Louis Armstrong back from the dead to remind us "What a Wonderful World" we live in, another Merle Haggard, another wants Tupac in holograph-form breaking down "Only God Can Judge Me," and many of the answers are personal, not grand—a sister or best friend singing "Over the Rainbow."

Torrie Fields, a palliative-care advocate, answered this question like she had been rehearsing it for decades, and it turns out she has. "My mom would sing Billy Joel's 'Vienna,'" she said. "And when the second verse starts, my best friends would start singing the Beatles' 'Let It Be.'" The two bookend each other, she explained. "'Vienna' is the song that has summed up my life. 'Let It Be' I hope is how I am remembered."

It isn't common for someone to assign the singing part to a parent. One of the few orders we all try to follow in the universe is that a child should outlive the parent. But Torrie was diagnosed with stage 2 cervical cancer when she was only nineteen and had seven surgeries in three years. Though she was in remission, the cancer came back when she was twenty-nine. Now she's thirty-two, and the cancer is again in remission, for now.

"Vienna," which is tattooed on Torrie's right hip, was the song her mom sang to her as a child. "My mom's obsessed with Billy

Joel, which means I am obsessed with Billy Joel. Instead of nursery rhymes, she sang Billy Joel to me." "Vienna" was the most fitting song for Torrie, with its admonitions to "Slow down, you crazy child," and "you can't be everything you want to be before your time."

"I was always this crazy kid who was running, running, running as fast as possible," she said. "If I'd slowed down, I would have fallen apart, so I just kept running."

"Having cancer was the best thing that ever happened to me," she said. "It oriented me, taught me what mattered. Showed me who mattered, and I found out who I am." Torrie's mom always said that "Vienna" must have been written for her daughter. "The song taught me to honor old age and death. That there is something beyond productivity. No matter what happens, you don't have to prove that you are productive; you only have to prove that you're a good person. I would hope that my friends would retain that memory of me. Not the running, running, running." That's why "Let It Be," sung by her friends, would be the perfect response to "Vienna." Torrie wanted her friends to think of her as having transcended the need to be *doing* all the time.

I asked if she'd thought about what it would be like for her mom and her friends to sing in that context. "I imagine they'd fall apart," I offered.

"Yeah, and that's okay," she said. "It's almost the beauty of it, to fall apart. It is okay to fall apart to these songs. I've devoted a lot of my life to create better spaces for grief in my community and friend group. I've found, over time, that the more I'm able to create these spaces for grief, where I can name my grief, the more open people are to share theirs. I can only hope my death would reflect that."

The music profession is obviously filled with bright shiny stars, names we recognize, music we know by heart. Behind the names are the producers, managers, songwriters, folks who shape and sculpt the music and musical careers that mean so much to us. There are few behind-the-scene players who have been more influential in the past twenty years than Richard Nichols. Many know him as the manager of The Roots, but that single description does nothing to account for the number of artists he mentored, inspired, collaborated with, challenged, pissed off, pushed, and cajoled until they found their authentic voice.

After Richard Nichols died of leukemia, Questlove from The Roots wrote, "Our culture calls for certain forms of expression in the wake of an event like this: We're supposed to compose a declaration of devotion to the departed, offer testimony regarding his lasting importance, make a simple statement of the sadness that has settled over us all. There is no declaration or testimony big enough to fill the life of Rich. But there is a simple statement, and this is it: There is only one Richard Nichols. I know what ya'll are thinking: 'There is only one of each of us.' But it's truer than true in this case."[1]

When Rich was diagnosed with leukemia he created a new twitter handle—@coolhandleuk—filled with his thoughts on treatment and his eventual death. Rich was a modern-day stoic philosopher, always seemingly ready to face whatever difficulty life threw at him. Even though Rich was at peace with his encroaching death, his closest community couldn't wrap their heads around a world without Rich. Ginny Suss, who has worked closely with The Roots for over fifteen years in various capacities, from production to tour management, and more recently was the producer of the Women's March and founder of the Resistance Revival Chorus, had this to say: "He'd been sick and then recovered before. It felt like he was indestructible. It didn't feel like he was really going to leave us. And then I got a call that said, 'You'd better come down. We're taking him off support.' I jumped in my car and immediately got a flat tire. So I had to get the tire fixed, then drove six hours down to Philly in a state of grief and shock."

Rich, in his final weeks, had created a final show, his memorial, with a program for a three-hour ceremony that was detailed down to the minute. After Rich died, his assistant, Alexis, informed the artists that Rich had scripted what songs he wanted, who should sing them, and at what times they should be prepared to perform. Ginny reflected on this months after Rich's death: "He produced the way everyone would process his death. As a producer he produced his way out of this world. He was offering a healing ceremony."

Emily Wells, a profoundly talented violinist and composer, met Rich only a couple of years before he died but developed an immediate familial and creative bond with him. She got the same call as Ginny and found herself included in a small group of people near Rich when he died. A week afterward she got another call: Rich had written her into his memorial celebration. He'd wanted her to perform.

Emily recounted the rite of passage that everyone encountered after entering Union Transfer, a venue in Philadelphia. "You walk in—there's one entrance, and there's a long table with wooden boxes and this fertile, dark soil. We had to put our hands into this soil, and then we had to all rinse our hands in the same water. We were all touching these elements from the same boxes and rinsing our hands in the same water, and it was a way of making us all one from the moment we arrived. That had a pretty striking effect on everyone entering because you realize this isn't your everyday funeral, and nobody's going to get away with being half here. And Rich got that out of people in life. He didn't have time for people being half present, so it made sense that his farewell was also like that. . . . I'd never experienced someone being so present at their own good-bye. It was so beautiful and so . . . brave and so fearless to stage that, and you felt that boldness."

I wanted to know if it was hard to perform a song for someone you love so much, thinking that some of us will be asked to do the same thing for a loved one someday. "It was not comfortable," Emily said. "But that's part of it, not being comfortable. I don't have a ton of experience with death, but I've never experienced something like that night, the buoyancy. I felt like we were all levitating. It felt like we were moving upward instead of downward. Everyone in the room, everyone on the stage. Musically speaking, it was divine. . . . And we all had to cooperate with each other to pull this off, even under the very strained circumstances of grieving, so that cooperation gave us something to do with our hands, so to speak."

"There were beautiful moments," said Ginny. "There's a song, 'Dear God,' one of the most beautiful Roots songs ever. And I think a lot of people will always remember that moment when it was sung."

Ginny talked about the hardship but also the gift of strengthened community that Rich left behind, "It was like a wedding. A birth. His passing was the birth of so many things for me. Sometimes in human nature we're afraid of change. But friendships were born; friendships were solidified."

"The next day I went to a studio and ended up writing a song called 'Richard,'[2] Emily said. "I didn't want to turn it off because I wasn't ready to come down. I played it on loop all day. I wanted to hold onto the experience."

Renee described her grandfather's funeral with a range of emotions, with a good amount of tension and uncertainty, much like the family's relationship with the man himself. "He was lovely, but I was also terrified of him," Renee said. His life had been so different from that of his children and grandchildren. He'd grown up on a farm during the Great Depression and had to leave school to work. He served in the Pacific arena during World War II, and when he returned, he took his role as provider very seriously. He was apt to lose his temper over things like leaving food uneaten and had complex relationships with his wife and children. He was not a man to be crossed. But he had a sly sense of humor, a brilliant mind, and a way with words that Renee bonded with him over. "When I was living in the UK," she remembered, "He wrote me letters with punny things like, kilts being 'daft/aft/draft.'"

The funeral was fraught for many reasons, one being that no one was sure how his wife of sixty years would be. She was dying herself, and she had been deeply angry that she'd been living in a nursing home, something Renee's grandfather had felt guilty about. Then there were the different relationships he'd had with all his children. How would one eulogy bring all of what he was together in a way that would feel satisfying and speak to everyone?

Renee's aunt took on the job. It felt appropriate. She had been the closest to her father, and as a former nun, then a UCC minister, and eventually a hospice chaplain, she was the type of person others gravitated to. She would know the right thing to say.

In the middle of her eulogy she stopped speaking and started singing. ("She has pretty tremendous pipes," Renee said.) A cappella, she burst into the Eddie Fisher song from 1954, "Oh! My Papa." "When she sang, 'To me he was so wonderful,'" Renee said, "there wasn't a dry eye in the joint."

Are you an organ donor?

"One day it was just me and my cardiologist in the room," said Bella. "It was a year after I had gotten my new heart, and she said, 'You know it wasn't your fault. You didn't do anything to deserve this. Or this responsibility.'"

Bella was nine when she learned she had a heart condition, and she was in high school when she had a cardiac arrest and a stroke. She was put on the transplant list before her eighteenth birthday, which gave her priority to get a new heart.

"I cried when my cardiologist said it wasn't my fault," said Bella, "but not because I didn't know that. I did. But to have someone say it out loud was really, really powerful."

Bella asked her cardiologist why she didn't have more teenagers to talk to who were also going through it. There were support groups for teenaged cancer patients—why not transplant patients?

"You know why," her cardiologist said. "Because they're dead."

Teenagers often rebel against taking the medications they need to keep their new organ working properly with the rest of their bodies, the medications that keep them alive. There is a very complicated equation at work for transplant recipients, and particularly for teenagers, it can be hard to reconcile. "Cancer is always bad news," said Bella, "but a life-saving transplant looks different. It's this awful experience. Someone has to die for you to live. But it comes with a miracle at the end. How do you hold that?"

Like other teenagers, Bella feels inclinations to rebel too. "I have a strong gag reflex from my time in the hospital," she explained. "Taking pills is a chore. And it's a stamp of being different. A reminder that I have to manage this." She often hears of kids who skip their meds or do other destructive things like using meth after a transplant. "I get it," she said. And though she would never do meth, she also said of the kids who do, "I don't think they're total idiots. Life after transplant is so much harder. Every single transplant recipient I've ever talked to is on antidepressants. If I go off my antidepressants, I feel it. I've thought, 'I'm living in someone's body that's not mine. I should have died.' I've talked to a lot of people who feel this way."

Bella moved into the hospital on a cold March day and stayed through her transplant in June. Those months were filled with visits from her friends, who meant well but lived in an entirely different universe from the one she inhabited. Her boyfriend sent frequent texts guilting her about petty stuff you'd expect from a seventeen-year-old boy who is horny, emotional, and completely out of his element. Her friends tried to keep her from being too isolated by keeping a group chat going with her. When they started writing about parties and games and events that Bella couldn't attend, though, she dropped out of the group. Her friends couldn't fathom what it was to face death. "Bella," one guy in the group wrote, "I've cried too much over you for you not to interact with me."

Before the transplant Bella didn't spend much time thinking about death. She was so sick that she spent long hours in bed just trying to manage her symptoms. Now that she has her new heart and is living a relatively normal life, she thinks about death all the time. "Whenever I have a symptom," she says, "I think, 'this is it.'" She knows that she will most likely have to have another transplant. She just doesn't know when. "It could be next year," she says. "It could be forty years. It *could* be never, but that's not likely. A donor heart never lasts that long. Maybe I'll get another one when I'm fifty. The longest I've ever heard of one lasting is thirty years."

And so Bella has this perpetual feeling of doom that she recognizes isn't exactly normal for a nineteen-year-old. But it comes with a level of liberation too. She wants to be a teacher and work with children and feels impervious to peer pressure on the subject. There's not a drive to make the most money or do the coolest, sexiest job. Being with kids is what she loves and is passionate about, and she has a wizened clarity about what matters. That, she said, is a form of enlightenment. When her friends talk about experimenting with drugs, how they "almost died" doing LSD or how they had an experience of enlightenment from the drug, Bella has no patience for it. "No, you didn't almost die," she says. "I did. And you have to earn that kind of enlightenment."

Bella reached out to the family of the young man whose heart now beats in her body. Six months later they wrote back to her. She learned they were in Anchorage, in the same town she had just visited for her uncle's funeral. This young stranger, by checking a box, gave Bella the greatest gift of her life. And also, possibly, the greatest burden.

In the seminal book *The Gift* by Lewis Hyde, we learn that when you buy and sell something, it creates a boundary, often a border. Clearly defined lines and borders are healthy and necessary for economics and for trade partners. A gift, however, has a completely different dynamic structure. Gifts create connection, dissolve boundaries, and tie us to each other.

This understanding of a gift is why I never charge for the death dinners I host. The dinner party is a gift—it is meant to create community, not economics. We get it so backward. I invite you to consider that economics rely on relationships and that relationships rely on trust. When we give or share ourselves vulnerably or authentically with someone, we build trust. You could argue that our entire culture rests on gifts and the trust that comes from them. No wonder we are culturally so unwell: we have put the economics at the *root*, not as the branch and fruit of the tree.

When you need an organ from someone, arguably the most valuable gift you can receive, it can become toxic in our world based upon commerce and transaction. This a tremendous burden to place on anyone, let alone a teenager. Our task is to surround these souls with human connection and allow them to "pay it forward"—and to practice gratitude, not be immobilized by the weight.

⁓

"Do you want to be an organ donor?" is such a prosaic question, asked most often during the annoying adult task of getting your driver's license issued or renewed. You take your number in the blandness of the DMV's fluorescent-lit waiting room, where everyone would rather be somewhere else. You fill out forms with information you've recorded hundreds of times—date of birth, address, emergency contact. You're asked to check off a box about your willingness to be an organ donor if the unthinkable happens. Perhaps you skip it, not wanting to think of it. Then you get on with your day.

When you stop for a moment and really *do* think about it, however, what is offered with the check of a box is extraordinary. What begins with the definition of prosaic ends with the miraculous—medically, anyway, if not psychically. And the significance of a simple checkmark grows even more complex when you consider that, perhaps more than any other life-and-death predicament, the world of organ-donorship gets very entangled in questions about worth.

When Rick Segal was diagnosed with a fatal heart condition in 2004, he learned that, first, he would need a new heart if he was going to survive and, second, only 12 percent of his fellow New Yorkers were registered organ donors. Whereas Bella got a heart almost immediately, it took five years for Rick to get one—five years that can really mess with a person. Because, of course, when you want to live and you need a heart transplant to do so, you are waiting for someone to die.

Rick was in a hospital bed at NY-Presbyterian when a flock of Canada geese flew into the engine of a US Airways flight. Many of us know the rest of the story: Captain Sully kept his head and saved hundreds of lives, and later Tom Hanks cemented Sully's hero status by playing him in the movie made about the incident. When he heard about the near-crash, Rick's first thought was, *There could have been a plane full of potential donors right next to my hospital.* And then he despaired that he'd had the thought in the first place. As Rick's son, Greg, explains, "Cancer patients may tell you that they hate their chemo; organ transplant waiting list patients will tell you that they hate themselves."

Happily, Rick did get a donor at the eleventh hour, and a decade later he's thriving. The transplant came after five years of hell for him and his family, five years of him being terribly sick, five years of him wondering why only 12 percent of New Yorkers thought his life was worth saving.

There are understandable reasons why people don't sign up as organ donors. Some have opposition to it because of their religion. (Of note: many Catholic leaders see organ donation as a permissible final act, and Pope Emeritus Benedict XVI donated an organ when he was a cardinal.) Others, particularly marginalized populations, don't trust the system and are reluctant to put their name on any sort of registry, let alone one that has physically invasive implications. But unlike other medical issues, the world of transplants relies on people to participate in the system. It relies on the kindness of strangers.

Rick's son Greg felt this factor was perhaps the hardest during those long years of waiting. "I was walking around a place where I felt like nobody gave a f**k," Greg said. Friends would check in with him and ask how he was doing, how he was handling the crisis with his dad, and if there was anything they could do. In response to the last, he'd say, "Yeah, register as an organ donor." And people didn't. Or wouldn't. "That made all their sympathy feel hollow," Greg said. Of course he wasn't asking anyone directly to give his dad a heart—he was asking for a symbolic gesture of their generosity and understanding. But when people didn't rise to the question, he stopped asking, and he stopped talking about it. "It was too painful to have that experience. I felt like people didn't care to do something that was literally costless."

After Rick received his transplant, the effect it had on Greg's life did not abate. His chosen profession was venture capital, but at night he'd lose sleep thinking about organ donation. When his dad was sick he had often wondered why organ donor organizations didn't make more use of families like his in their advocacy work. He wondered a lot of things about the system that, from his observations, was badly broken. "I kept wondering how we could get more people organ transplants and who I knew who might fund it or partner with us. I was in a position where I was single, in my twenties, no kids. And if you're in that position and you're able, you spend money and time on what you can't sleep about. So I recognized, I have to do this. I can't talk myself out of it."

Greg cofounded Organize, a nonprofit committed to transforming the world of organ donation. He and his partner, Jenna Arnold, started the first central organ donor registry and advocate to make everything donor-related easier, more streamlined, and completely demystified. A critical part of that work is getting our society to think differently about checking off a box. Organize aims to take the conversation away from the DMV (which, as we've established, everyone hates) and into a forum where it's neither onerous nor scary: social media. As anathema as it might seem to hashtag your donor wishes, it's actually legit. Greg and Jenna went back to the men who, in the 1960s, were responsible for instituting the ways we express our organ donor wishes and challenged them to update how people register as organ donors. Far from scoffing at formats like Twitter and Facebook, they endorsed these platforms as the logical place to publicly make your donor wishes known.

The upshot of all this is that you can now easily express your desires to be an organ donor. Greg and Jenna have also launched Give and Live, a living donor site aimed at kidney donation. Give and Live got an initial push when it was featured on *Last Week Tonight* with John Oliver. Oliver skewered the expensive and dangerous dialysis business, comparing dialysis centers to Taco Bells. He also made an appeal for people to tweet their willingness to donate: #WhenIDiePleaseTakeMyKidneys. Oliver's segment got millions of views on YouTube and sparked a social media trend. The number of people who signed up in a single day to donate a kidney was greater than the total number of kidneys that had been donated in thirty years. The next month the White House, under President Obama, held its first summit on organ donation. Change is afoot, and it's an incredible thing.

We have a very solvable problem before us. If the majority of people registered to be organ donors, then we would not have a shortage. We would not have a five-year waiting list. We would not have the pain and suffering that came from Rick's long years of waiting, Greg's feeling that his fellow New Yorkers had abandoned him, or Bella's grappling with the worthiness of her young life. And it's costless. Huge upside, no downside. If someone has a strong faith that forbids them from donating an organ, that's one thing. But those who opt not to be donors comprise a much greater portion of the population. They decline not out of a religious or moral objection but because they don't want to think about it. Because it's easy to just check no or opt not to check anything off at all. And here Greg's feelings of abandonment make perfect sense: all you really need to do is acknowledge that you *will* die one day—and it's the fear of looking at that unequivocal truth that gets in the way.

What does a good death look like?

The plan, Kathy Maxwell explained, was to go out for dinner after her mother's appointment with her doctor. Kathy's three siblings were in town, and they were looking forward to going to a Greek restaurant that was her mother's favorite. No one really expected bad news at that appointment. Kathy's mom, Tudy, was generally in excellent health. Yes, she'd had some achiness on a hike, which had precipitated the appointment, but how many other people in their midseventies were hiking the way she was in the first place? And she looked fantastic—a picture of health.

The doctor set them all straight. She sat the family down and explained that the melanoma for which Tudy'd previously been given the all-clear was back and that the cancer had spread everywhere. Solemnly, the doctor told Tudy to get her affairs in order, that she had six weeks to six months left. She died five weeks from that very day.

As the family walked out into the parking lot, the siblings were a wreck, none knowing what to do next.

"We're going to go out for dinner!" Tudy pronounced. And so they did, all pushing food around their plates in shock.

"My sister had a guest cottage, and I moved into it with my mom," Kathy said. "All the grandkids came to say good-bye. And my daughter, Rosie, took a semester off of college so that she could come help."

Tudy had a great team caring for her. Kathy herself was a nurse, they had hospice involved, and Rosie was physically strong, which proved instrumental, as she was able to move Tudy when it was needed. Rosie had brought Tudy's favorite book, *The Little Prince*, and spent afternoons reading it out loud to her. They also had time to talk. "Rosie had said to my mom, 'You're not going to be around for my wedding, for my children. How am I going to know you're with me?' And my mom said, 'I think I'll show up as hearts in unexpected places.' Rosie and I see hearts everywhere."

Two days before Tudy died, Rosie was sitting by her bed. Tudy was in a lot of pain, but all of a sudden she started moving her hands and said, "Oh! I'm just . . . I'm on this path, and it's beautiful! There are flowers. And a cat."

Rosie asked, "Is anyone there?"

"Yes," Tudy said. "My friend Judy." Rosie kept asking questions about what Tudy saw until Tudy finally said, "Honey, whenever you ask me a question I have to go back to the beginning of the path."

"It was as if she was walking into a family reunion," Kathy remembered. "She was animated and happy to see everyone. When she came out of that space, she asked for her little black book, where she kept recipes and notes to herself, and she wrote 'Maryan' in it. She said, 'I want Maryan to be the one to get me.'" Maryan was Tudy's older sister, who Tudy had adored and who had died at just thirty-three.

Rosie continued reading *The Little Prince* to her grandma, and on what would be Tudy's last day, Rosie and Kathy took turns reading chapters until they'd finished. That night Rosie asked Kathy, "Do you mind if I come up and sleep with Grandma and you?"

They tucked Tudy in, and she died that night.

"My mom lived life being afraid of a lot of things," Kathy said. "She didn't believe she had the talent to do much except raise kids and make meals and do laundry. But she is someone who died with more elegance and grace than I'd ever seen."

"Fuck ME! You weren't kidding—that was bitter!"

Lester hollered, his substantial baritone echoing through his sister's house as he reached for water. Crown Royal had been Lester's comforter and captor for much of his adult life, but this was the first shot he had thrown back in years.

In Washington State, if you choose to end your life via death with dignity, the capsules of meds are emptied and mixed with water, fruit juice, or a liquor drink of choice. Most recovering alcoholics don't choose alcohol as the substrate for the concoction that will quickly dim their consciousness until it slips away—they don't want the booze to get any limelight in their final moments. But Lester thought there was a great irony in the Crown Royal and saw the humor in the whole situation.

The table erupted with laughter and then tears as Sally McLaughlin told this story on a dark, wintry, rain-pelted evening on the banks of Lake Washington in perhaps the coziest home I have ever visited. We were eating Chicken Marbella, a classic from the *Silver Palate Cookbook*. The table had another opportunity to laugh when I'd asked, "What's Chicken Marbella?" I was by far the youngest person at the table; the average age of my other dinner companions was pushing seventy. (I guess if you're seventy, you know the dish.)

I had been invited over to host a death dinner with the board of directors of End of Life Washington, a group that helps people plan for the final days of their lives. The nonprofit counsels clients on all their end-of-life options, including a planned death, and advocates for choices for the terminally ill. Our table included one of the organization's founders and one of the early pioneers in the assisted-death movement, Sheila Cook (pronounced "Shilah,"

I was told with firm sweetness), aged eighty-seven. This was a group of humans who knew the grim reaper better than almost anyone, and I wanted to know a death they had experienced that qualified as "good."

Sally is the executive director of End of Life Washington. The organization trains volunteers to administer the necessary medications, and the first death Sally witnessed with the organization, when she was still just a volunteer and not the director, was an unequivocally good one, she said. She was grateful. Although intellectually she believed it was right for people to be able to end their own lives when they were sick, emotionally she was uncertain about how it would feel to witness.

Which brings us back to Lester and his Crown Royal.

It all started with Lester's sister, Mary. She and Lester hadn't been in touch for seventeen years, but when their stepmother died, Mary found Lester, who was living in a trailer home somewhere in Georgia, and told him the news. "What a coincidence," Lester said. "I'm dying too." He had stage 4 bone cancer.

Lester had had a rough life. A recovering alcoholic, he described himself as a construction worker, but no one was sure how or how well he got by. Mary and her brother had a difficult past together, but she could not accept that he might die alone in a trailer in Georgia that might not have running water or electricity. She brought him to live with her in Washington State, and they called End of Life Washington soon afterward to talk about options for hastened death.

On their first meeting, after Lester got an overview of what the whole process would look like, Sally noticed that he looked unsettled. Sally asked, "Lester, do you have some questions?"

"Yes," he said. "I was kind of wondering what happens after."

"To your body? Or are you wondering what will happen to Lester once he's no longer in his body?"

"Yeah," he said. "That's what I'm wondering." Sally talked with Lester about enrolling in a hospice program and how, if he wished, he could have a chaplain come and speak to him.

A week or so later Sally heard from Lester's sister Mary, who said Lester was feeling upset and would love another visit from Sally. "I wasn't sure exactly what I was going to say or do," Sally said, "but I thought, 'I'm going to just talk to Lester as one human being to another.'"

As they began to talk about Lester's concerns about death, he said, "You know, I just think of my mother and my grandmother. They were blessed women filled with faith, and then I think of my life and how I've lived it, and it just . . ." He was quiet for a while, and Sally let the silence be. "What I'm kind of hoping," he finally continued, "is that when I go to that light, at the other end of the tunnel I find a grassy knoll in the sunshine with a cup of coffee and a guitar."

"That's just what we're going to envision for you then," Sally said. Then she added, "You know, there was something crazy Steve Jobs reportedly said as he was dying that gives me hope. Apparently, his last words were 'Oh wow. Oh wow, oh wow,' which he said in increasing tones of amazement and joy." Lester's eyes got big. "I don't know about you," Sally added, "but I'm really curious to know what Steve Jobs was experiencing."

Lester's energy shifted at that point, and he and Sally started talking about his acoustic guitar, which was on the wall beside his bed. When he learned that Sally played, he asked her to play a little for him. They talked animatedly about the music of Chet Atkins, Keb Mo, and John Prine. Although he was in a lot of pain, Lester sat up, took the guitar from Sally, and began to play the hell out of that guitar. Sally had spent some time playing in a band and was a pretty good musician herself, but though Lester was in pain and on morphine, he played better than she ever had.

"What's your favorite Chet Atkins song?" Sally asked.

"Vincent," he said, with no hesitation. Sally was moved, as the song about Vincent van Gogh was one of her favorites too. "I don't know why I did it," Sally said, "because it's not like me, but I just started singing it. And he started singing with me."

Sally and Lester were dramatically different people, from different backgrounds, whose paths would not have crossed but for these unusual circumstances. Sally is a highly educated lesbian living in a metropolitan area of the Northwest, and Lester had struggled with poverty and alcoholism for most of his life in the rural South. But on that day they were two musicians, bonding.

Before she left, Sally said, "I'm going to create a playlist for when I come back." There was no need to be more explicit. They both knew the circumstances in which she would be back. "I'll put Keb Mo, Chet Atkins, and Johnny Prine on it."

"Put some stuff you like on it too," Lester offered.

"No, this is your party."

He then tried to give Sally his guitar.

"I can't take your guitar."

"Why not?" he asked.

"Think about it. We have a great connection, but we just started talking forty-five minutes ago, and now you want me to leave here with your most prized possession?"

Lester laughed. "I guess you're right."

"But the thought you'd offer it to me means the world. Thank you."

Not long after, Lester's sister called and said he was ready. His pain medications weren't working anymore, he was suffering, and he was ready to go. And so it was that on a cold, drizzly early January morning Sally went out to Lester's house one last time.

Sally sat with Lester and his sister while a colleague prepared the medication prescribed by his physician. Only Lester himself was permitted to administer it. First he took some antinausea medication, which needed to be consumed forty-five minutes before he could take the meds that would end his life. While they waited, Sally and Lester listened to the playlist she'd made for him, and they talked with Mary—not a music aficionado herself—about what was so great about each of the songs.

"He was really energized and relaxed by the music," Sally said. "When the medication was ready, I told him, but I also said, 'Lester, you don't have to take it. In fact, you don't have to do any of this.'

"But Lester said, 'Let's get 'er done.'" He tossed back the drink, cursing up a storm when it touched his lips.

"His sister sat in one chair and I sat in another. He told me to turn the music up. A John Prine song was playing: *We had an apartment in the city, me and Loretta liked living there.* Then Lester reached for his guitar and started playing along, and I started singing. He started singing the harmonies with me. And I thought, 'This guy isn't going to die. He has way too much life energy.'"

But he stopped playing, rested his hand on the fretboard, and closed his eyes.

Before arriving at Lester's that day Sally had felt unsettled. She had converted to Catholicism years before, then drifted far from the cloth. She knew that by being a part of Lester's death, she would be forever changed. What if the Church was right? What if what she was doing was wrong? But as she sat with Lester, she felt the moment was so dignified, gentle, and beautiful. She didn't feel she'd committed some mortal sin.

"I put my hand on his," Sally said, "and said, 'God bless you,' and I left."

His sister texted Sally afterward: "Wasn't that the perfect way for Lester to leave? I doubt you will come across many DWD [death with dignity] clients who swallow the meds, then casually reach up, lift a guitar off the wall, and start playing and singing. What a memory to have. Thank you."

One of Sally's most vivid impressions of the experience was that she met Lester at a time when he was facing his fears— not about dying but about what comes after death. "Well, now he knows," she said. Lester set the benchmark for the work that Sally has done since and enables her to do it in a way that is confident rather than ambivalent. To Sally, to his sister Mary, and to Lester, it was a beautiful death.

What do you want done with your body?

Scott Kreiling is one of the most influential healthcare professionals in the west, though he is so humble that he would never describe himself that way. Yet even though he is the president of Regence BlueShield Idaho and a director at the Cambia Health Foundation, he realized he didn't have any idea what his aging parents wanted during their last years, days, or after they had passed. His relationship with his stoic father was challenging at times. So it was with trepidation that Scott flew from Boise to Tucson to ask his parents a series of questions about advanced care, what their end-of-life goals might look like, and what they wanted done with their bodies.

Scott's mother said she wanted her ashes spread on Oregon's nascent volcano, Mt. Hood, near the historic Timberline Lodge. But then the dialogue shifted, and what emerged was a clear picture that he hadn't been able to ascertain before. Scott saw that his mother was exhibiting unmistakable signs of early-onset Alzheimer's, and the burden was weighing heavily on Scott's father. In a dramatic turn of events, Scott quickly identified that his mother needed a full-time care facility and that even his father needed some assistance in his regular day-to-day life, and then he asked them if they wanted to move to Boise. Within a month they had packed the family car and set out across the Western Plains. His mother and father took up residence in an independent living facility for the first year and a half, with assistance from caregivers, and then ultimately lived in separate care facilities and visited each other several times a week. They also spent ample time with their grandchildren, Scott, and his wife.

As his mother's health began to deteriorate even further, Scott once again revisited her wishes with his dad. But there had been so much focus on his mom that Scott realized he still didn't know what his father wanted. He knew he wanted to be cremated, but not what he wanted done with his ashes. So over burgers and beer at Red Robin, he asked.

"That's a good question," Scott's dad said. "I haven't really thought about it. I guess I figured you would want to just sit there and stare at them. . . . What are my choices?"

Two years prior Scott would never have had this conversation with his father. They had a difficult time talking about ordinary things, let alone death and legacy.

"You have a lot of choices," Scott said. "You're a pilot, you're a boater, a golfer . . ."

There was a long pause before Scott's father asked quietly, "Can you throw them outside of an airplane over the Boise Foothills?"

"We can do that," Scott said.

After that conversation Scott's dad would regularly remind him about the airplane and the ashes, as if making sure his wish was really going to be honored.

One January day Scott got a text that his mom was in distress and was being put on oxygen. He stopped everything and rushed to her bedside. "She knew who I was, even with her advanced Alzheimer's. I played music for her, I told her stories and showed her pictures, I said a prayer for her, I told her we all loved her and that if she wanted to go that it was okay. She turned and looked at me, squeezed my hand, smiled, and stopped breathing." Three days later Scott's father, who had no heart issues to speak of, had a heart attack and died within minutes. This summer Scott and his sister will be meeting up to celebrate their father and honor his wishes.

The experience with his parents changed Scott's approach to end-of-life issues. He has become one of the most prolific leaders in the space, gathering dozens of the most powerful CEOs in Idaho to engage in death dinners, holding summits to change the care models in Boise and across the state, and leading the charge at Cambia—the largest insurance provider across Washington, Idaho, Utah, and Oregon—as the pioneer in end-of-life conversations.

What I take from Scott's story is that even those who are professionally involved in healthcare are not asking the questions of the people closest to them. And through his courage and a simple set of questions, Scott was able to identify his mother's condition, ask his parents if they wanted to be closer to him and their grandchildren, provide appropriate care for both of his parents, reduce their suffering, improve his relationship with his dad, and identify his father's wishes so that Scott could meaningfully honor him after his death.

I think of the dull ache that his parents' deaths would have caused in Scott if he hadn't done the work. There is no question that he is navigating a serious amount of grief with the consecutive loss of both of his parents, but it's clear that there is meaning in this grief, not just a wall of pain. When we don't know how to honor our loved ones, it adds immense confusion to devastating loss and elongates the healing process. If we know of a clear ritual to honor their legacy, if we know their desires, we have a powerful role to play.

Nearly 80 percent of India's population identify as Hindu, which is over a billion people, or one-seventh of the world's population. So when we discuss the death rituals in India, it is not a small discussion but rather something that impacts a large portion of our globe—even larger when you consider the diaspora: Indian immigrants are the second-largest community of first-generation immigrants in the United States.

These statistics, like all statistics, are connected like fine filament to actual human hearts. Alpa Agarwal was at her desk at Microsoft's headquarters in Redmond, Washington, when she received the call that her father had fallen deathly ill. Within forty-eight hours she was in Mumbai, India, by her father's bedside. He was in and out of consciousness. After a life of alcoholism, several of his organs were beginning to fail. Alpa was with him when he died.

Performing the last rites at a Hindu cremation ceremony is a forbidden act for a woman. The Vedas, or religious texts, are crystal clear on this point. The eldest son is responsible, and if there is no son in the family, a male cousin or uncle is meant to step in. There is no room in the ceremony for a daughter. Women are expressly forbidden to even attend Shamshan Ghaat, the ritual cremation grounds.

The last rites, like death itself, are a powerful combination of the tender and the coarse. One Hindu custom calls for gold coins to be placed in the eye sockets, rice placed in the hands, and flowers adorning the body—all symbols of abundance waiting for the deceased on their karmic journey. The body is cremated in an open pyre and attended to with prayer and mantras. Then comes the Kapal Kriya, which is perhaps the most brutal-sounding act to the Western ear. It is the act of crushing the deceased's skull midcremation with an eight-foot-long bamboo joust. This is not an easy task—emotionally, or physically. At this point in the cremation the head is often obscured under piles of wooden logs and ash from flowers and skin.

The skull is crushed for several reasons, ranging from practical to mystical. The cavity won't fully burn in an open pyre without being broken into pieces. It is also believed that the soul is held in the area of the third eye, behind the forehead, and this merciful gesture allows it freedom as it journeys to its next incarnation. There is an even more occult layer, and many believe that a skull can be possessed if dark spirits find it intact.

Alpa decided that she would perform the last rites, oversee the ceremony, and be the one to crush her father's skull. If her brother had been in Mumbai, he would have joined her in equal participation. Her more traditional dad's side of the extended family tried to stop her, while her less traditional mother's side encouraged and helped her. Alpa remembers looking at her deceased father's face, asking what he wanted. When Alpa was growing up, her father had been stuck between the traditional and the modern. But deep in her heart she knew he wanted her to perform his last rites. Alpa had to prostrate herself on the floor in front of the priest many times and cajole him to get his permission to perform these traditionally patriarchal duties. The negotiation went on for a few hours as the body was being prepared. But it was worth it. The tears that drenched Alpa's face during the entire twelve-hour-long ceremony gave her an opportunity to fully grieve her father.

Ritual is a powerful and imperfect science. Ritual and death have been fused for the entire history of mankind. Nowhere is it clearer than in relationship to how we treat the bodies of our dead loved ones. As we consider what we want, it is important to realize that we are pulling from thousands of years of tradition.

In *The Power of Myth* Joseph Campbell said, "A ritual is the enactment of a myth. And, by participating in the ritual, you are participating in the myth. And since myth is a projection of the depth wisdom of the psyche, by participating in a ritual, participating in the myth, you are being, as it were, put in accord with that wisdom, which is the wisdom that is inherent within you anyhow. Your consciousness is being re-minded of the wisdom of your own life."

Campbell may take this conversation too far afield for some. But Alpa knew what she needed to reckon with the death of her father, and sometimes it takes great courage to ask for what we need.

~

Katrina Spade, founder of Recompose—which, you might recall, converts human remains into soil—has heard scores of stories from people who have had horrible or confused experiences of burying a loved one. "Typically I hear, 'I went to the funeral home. And I wanted something simple. But they made me feel like I was dishonoring my mother because I wasn't going to buy the casket,'" Katrina said. "Another person told me, 'I had to have my sister embalmed because it's the law.' I know it's not the law," Katrina added, "but I don't want to say, 'You were duped. You were taken advantage of.'"

I have no desire to vilify the funeral industry, nor does Katrina. Most people working in it are compassionate and want to do right by their clients. But it must also be said that the funeral business is in trouble. While most funeral homes offer both cremation and embalming/burial, the cremation rate has grown dramatically and is estimated to hit 70 percent by 2030. Because the revenue for a cremation is just one-quarter of what it is for a burial, the math is pretty clear. Add to this that strict regulations keep the funeral industry from being as adaptable as it needs to be (they can't always offer green burial options, for instance), and you have economic stress.[1] And where you have economic stress, you have sales pressure.

The point is: know before you go. Be an educated consumer—whether you're planning for your own death or grappling with someone else's. And you don't just have two choices anymore. Cremation and funeral-home burials remain the most common practices in the United States, but people all over the world are reimagining what is possible, remembering what used to be practiced, and choosing an option that aligns with their core values.

One option is green burials. Brian Flowers is the general manager of The Meadow, a natural burial ground in northern Washington State. The basic idea with The Meadow and other green burial sites is that the body is returned to the earth, where its nutrients are cycled back into life-producing organisms. The body nourishes the soil, allowing plants and trees to grow from it. Brian's perspective is that with the popularity of cremation, we've lost the ritual in death. He points out that for thousands of years our ancestors gathered together to carry the dead to rest. There can be meaning in the physical act of carrying someone. There can be comfort in turning over the soil. It is a physical grieving that he argues you lose when you lose the physical body. And we can use the funeral walk to heal. He vividly remembers a burial he attended where a Buddhist staff was used in the procession. Every third step the staff hit the ground and bells clanged. The bells reminded those in the entourage to stay in the present. "Our ancestors spent as much as 70 percent of their time on ritual," he said. "Ritual matters."[2]

Marcus Daly is a coffin maker. The first coffin he ever built was for his own child when his wife had a miscarriage. In a powerful video he describes how personal it feels to have your hands on the wood, to work with it, to sand and sand and sand, and how, as with life, you never feel that you're fully done. "Benedictine monks say work and pray, and I guess those bleed together for me," he said. Like Brian Flowers, he finds great meaning in the physicality of grieving. "I think one of the most important aspects of the coffin is that it can be carried. And we're meant to carry each other. I think carrying someone you love and committing them is very important for us, and when we deal with death, we want to know that we have played a part and that we have shouldered our burden. So if we make it too convenient, then we're depriving ourselves of a chance to get stronger so that we can carry on."[3]

Katrina, too, grasps the importance of ritual—the physical and the symbolic—in death care. Her organization Recompose isn't only planning to provide a new form of disposition; it's also working to create a more expanded experience for the grieving. When someone dies, the family will be encouraged to take part in the care and preparation, washing and shrouding the body with help from specially trained staff. After the shrouding the body will be placed in an individual "vessel" with carbon-rich material, like woodchips. Through a natural process of microbial activity, the body decomposes rapidly—in just thirty days it has become soil. Families are then welcome to take the soil and use it to nourish a garden or a memorial tree—thus engaging in ritual again.

I know, some of you are now completely disgusted. But as Katrina points out, "If you want an *ick* factor, look into the modern embalming process—it has way more ick." For Katrina, who grew up in the New Hampshire countryside and has always felt deeply connected to the cycles of nature, decomposition makes perfect sense and aligns with her environmental values.

And then there is the Infinity Burial Suit. Developed by two designers, it is a shroud created from thread infused with mushroom spores. Mushrooms have the uncanny ability to absorb toxins. When you are laid to rest in a mushroom suit, then none of the lead or pesticides in your body get recycled back into the earth. You might wonder who would ever choose this option, to be consumed by mushrooms, but as it turns out the founder Jae Rhim Lee has been awash with people signing up. Her company, Coeio, has already had success with the Forever Spot, a pet-focused version of the mushroom suit that enables pet owners to shroud or wrap their pet in a bio-mix of mushrooms and other organisms and then bury their pet themselves.

Bios Urns will use your ashes to help grow a tree after you die. Algordanza, a company based in Chur, Switzerland, will apply thousands of pounds of pressure to your ashes for thousands of dollars, turning you into a diamond, a very shiny kind of immortality. Cremation Solutions will store your ashes in a customized action figure—you can add a cape or be memorialized in a cat woman outfit.

If all of this information makes you question your allegiance to environmentalism or sounds like a booth you might find at Comic-Con, fair enough. Traditional burial and cremation are still far and away the most common choices people make when it comes to their remains. And no one is to say what another finds meaningful. Kathy Maxwell, who you met on page 139, got together with her siblings after her mother was cremated and divided her ashes among them. "I took part of my allotment of her ashes and buried them in Iowa a year after she died, next to the spot where her mother and grandmother were buried. And then I realized I wanted part of my ashes buried there too when it was time, so I had a footstone made for myself.

"My sister took her to Pebble Beach," Kathy continued. "My brother Charlie has her in his office. My other brother has her in his living room. I sprinkled some in India, and in the lake near the resort in Colorado where she worked during high school, and some under the lemon tree in my yard. She's kind of all over, and that feels as it should be."

Cremation or burial, natural burial or funeral home, mushroom suit or lemon tree—the work here is in examining what matters to you and what matters to your loved ones. We need access to the multitude of information and options so we can embark on the self-reflective process of identifying what we want. On voting day I would never want half of a ballot.

Cassandra Yonder lives on a self-sustaining homestead in Cape Breton, Nova Scotia. At any given moment you'll find her throwing bales of hay, milking goats, or, alongside her children, processing chickens into meat. As the daughter of a veterinarian, it's a natural, comfortable world for her. She is there when her animals give birth, and she helps them achieve a good death. She is also someone with a lifelong comfort around grief—partly, she thinks, because her mother's mother died at the time she was conceived. "I believe my womb was a place of grief. My mom's grief for her mom was healthy, and it was a part of me." Cassandra's interest in the subject only grew, and when she was older, after obtaining degrees in sociology, gerontology, and architecture, she studied grief and bereavement.

Perhaps that's why what happened with her beloved neighbor Jeremy's postdeath care felt so right. Jeremy was a farmer, a poet, and a community activist. When his wife, Sue, was asked what kind of funeral he'd want, Sue didn't hesitate: he would want to be buried at home, on his property. He wouldn't want to hire services that could be done by family and friends.

This launched Cassandra into full-on "home funeral" research mode. From Jeremy's kitchen table she called coroners, the municipalities, local funeral providers, the medical examiner. What was possible? How could they manage this? When friends asked how they could help, Cassandra assigned them tasks. Several built a casket for Jeremy in his own woodshop. Several drove to the medical examiner's to retrieve Jeremy's body after the autopsy and bring it home. The old farm truck became a hearse. They had a wake at Jeremy's farmhouse, a service the next day at the church, and then a tractor led the mourners' way through the snow back to Jeremy's property and, ultimately, to the spot Sue had chosen for his grave, near where Jeremy's horse Whiskey was buried. Everyone took turns shoveling dirt into his grave, and they passed whiskey—the drink—around.

The experience, Cassandra said, was beautiful and important—everything from making those calls in his kitchen to shoveling dirt into his grave was a vital part of the grieving process. It was community building and, above all, empowering. Ultimately it led Cassandra to start a virtual school for community death-care in Canada. To Cassandra, community deathcare—or coming together to care for our dead without unnecessary medical and/or industrial intervention—is all about *reclaiming* care of our dying, dead, and bereaved.

"I see such a strong parallel between this movement and the slow food movement," Cassandra said. "What I see happening and the reason the slow food movement exists is that people go to the store and see cut-up bits of flesh wrapped in cellophane, and they feel disturbed. Their kids don't understand where eggs come from or that pork comes from pig. They don't know what exactly bothers them but somehow know that the food didn't come here in a good way. People stand at the grocery store and become aware of this sense of alienation. And the human response to that is to seek those connections again. People want to at least have access to information about how their food was prepared. And the ultimate act of reclaiming is to grow your own food in your own backyard."

Cassandra believes the phenomenon is similar when it comes to end of life, postdeath care, and grief. There's an anger she sees toward the healthcare system and funeral industry. "It touches that same place of alienation," she said. "They see a funeral director or a palliative care team doing something and think, 'I should be more involved. But I don't know how.'" So Cassandra is a proponent of active reclaiming of the death and the burial process. "We need to break down myths about how death needs to happen and forge opportunities to connect again."

There is a growing trend in the United States and in Canada to offer families nonmedicalized guidance through the death process. Many practitioners call themselves death midwives or death doulas. In a slight departure, Cassandra's virtual course offers modules with names like, "Post Death Body Care" and "Celebrant Skills and Deathcare Rituals," but even as she is training others, she doesn't offer her services to take grieving families through the process in real time.

"A woman called me this summer, and she had the impression that that's what I did," Cassandra said. The woman's father had died, and she wanted to hire Cassandra to come over, help her wash her father, and walk her through the whole home funeral process.

"I never said no," said Cassandra, "but I said, 'It's possible to do this yourself.' I found out the woman was a nurse and more competent than me. Over a five-day period we had daily conversations, and in the end I wasn't invited to the funeral, which was the greatest honor." The daughter held his funeral in his barn, and he was buried on his property. "She got what she needed from me," said Cassandra. "She realized it was her story."

Are there certain deaths we should never speak of?

With someone who has lived a long life, you can celebrate that life. But if someone's journey has just begun, where is the celebration in its end? If it's hard to talk about death with an eighty-year-old whose decline is evident, it feels like forbidden territory for an eight-year-old with a terminal illness. There are no words. The simple no that resounds through us is captured by this line from the musical *Hamilton*, "You hold your child as tight as you can. And push away the unimaginable." Childhood death is the final frontier of what we cannot and do not want to face. There is a strong instinct to hide it away because it's so painful. But we must consider what healing happens when we look at it directly. I think death pioneer Stephen Levine said it best: "When your fear touches someone's pain, it becomes pity, when your love touches someone's pain, it becomes compassion."[1]

Lynette Johnson takes photographs of children who are very sick, most of them dying. She and her team lovingly put together a handmade booklet of the photos for each family. This is not your average keepsake; these are objects of extraordinary craft and beauty. It is a gift, a memorial, and an important emotional record. For years other photographers would constantly say to her, "I don't know how you do it. I couldn't." She responded, "What are you talking about? You can do what's right. If it's presented to you, of course you can do it." She went from being the only photographer to the founder of a nonprofit dedicated to this work, Soulumination. In addition to taking photos of sick children, they also take photos of terminally ill adults with their young children. Sixty photographers now work with Soulumination in Seattle alone, and Lynette has given these volunteers encouragement to not only look at but also document the unimaginable.

Lynette didn't seek out this particular niche. It was presented to her, and she showed up. Over twenty years ago her sister-in-law lost her full-term baby in utero. Shockingly, the hospital sent her home—still heavily pregnant—and scheduled the delivery for the next day. Lynette's sister-in-law somehow had the presence of mind to ask Lynette to bring clothes for the baby to be cremated in once she was delivered and to be there to take photographs of the infant.

Lynette entered the room right after the delivery and presented a beautiful dress and bonnet that had been her own as a baby. The delivery nurse was callous—there's no other way to say it. She protested against having to clean and dress the baby and was very vocal about how hard it was to do because of the fragile state of the infant's skin. Her language was graphic, and her attitude was clear: you are making too big of a ritual over this. The father wasn't in the room at the time, and Lynette was frozen. The newly delivered mother, however, spoke up. "Shut up!" she yelled. "That is my baby you are talking about!" Lynette took a few photos, but the trauma of the scene kept her from taking more.

Five years later Lynette was hired to photograph a wedding and met with the couple beforehand to get to know them a little better. The bride worked at Seattle Children's Hospital, where she took care of very sick children. In the middle of the wedding planning meeting Lynette offered, "I can take photos for the families you work with, of their children," grasping the gravity of what she said only after it was out of her mouth. Her instincts had taken over, and the bride thought it was a beautiful idea. Lynette sighed, realizing that if she could take pictures for her sister-in-law, she could do it for anyone.

The gift these photographs are to families is hard to quantify. But Lynette—who is not religious—says that particularly when she photographs babies, she feels she's walking on holy ground. Often she is called when the decision has been made to remove the tubes that are keeping the baby alive. As the tape, tubes, wires, and signs of medical intervention are removed, the parents often see their child's face unencumbered for the first time. Lynette is present to capture it all, from their first breath on their own until their last.

Some might think, *Why would you want photographic reminders of the worst time in your life?* And yet the service Lynette offers is treasured. The evidence of how helpful it is comes in the thank-you notes Lynette receives. One parent wrote, "It is difficult to express exactly what these images of Mercer and our family mean to us. We are able to move forward never forgetting." Another wrote, "Today marks three years since my daughter's passing, with her fight against cancer, and I am truly grateful for you all, especially for putting together amazing keepsakes for my family to keep forever." And still another wrote, "[Our photos] perfectly show my beautiful, strong, raw, and imperfectly perfect baby girl. . . . Last year was so difficult for our family but you were there to capture our family's love and strength." It comes in the way so many parents come back to Lynette to volunteer their time or donate their money to her organization. And it comes in the stories they tell her. One parent said that she never goes to sleep without the box of photos Lynette took, which she keeps under her bed and within reach. If there is a fire in the middle of the night, she wants to be sure she can reach them.

The loss of a child is a grief so strong that the urge is to look away. But when you don't, when you face it instead, though you cannot take the pain away, you can bear witness. And that is something.

Many people say that they shy away from bringing up the loss of a child to a grieving parent. "I don't want to remind them," they say. But the parents are already thinking about it all the time. And when we turn away, we isolate them in their grief.

Greg Lundgren, who, you may recall, creates beautiful cast-glass and stone memorials and headstones, finds that his most frequent commissions come from bereaved parents. "I've seen people in their most vulnerable state," he said. "I've had mothers suggest their own suicide, who have said to me, 'If I can't finish this project, talk to my sister.' But I've seen how strong a human can be. I've seen people bury their husband and fall in love and get married again. I've seen people be suicidal and then I've seen them laughing. It's a testament to how strong the human spirit is and how people do recover." Greg also has the benefit of seeing these families intermittently, over a long period of time. "I don't see their grief minute to minute, hour to hour, but I have these sporadic check-in points, and I get to see it in these snapshots. I've witnessed a lot of people recover from grief. Not entirely, not completely, but I see their resilience. And that makes me stronger."

I know exactly what Greg means, and I know it because I know Dianne Gray.

Dianne is now the president of the Elisabeth Kübler-Ross Foundation. But before she started on this journey, she was on another one. Dianne's son Austin was four when he was diagnosed with a rare neurodegenerative disease called NBIA (neurodegenerative brain iron accumulation) disorder. She was told that he would go blind, that he would stop walking, and that he would die in two years. The disease progressed quickly, such that he went from walking unsteadily on a Tuesday to being wheelchair-bound by Friday. Within a few months he had trouble moving one arm. Then he couldn't put a fork to his mouth.

Dianne would take him on a "date night" to Barnes & Noble each week, and on one of these dates a book jumped off the shelf at her: *On Children and Death*, by Elisabeth Kübler-Ross. Dianne remembered studying Elisabeth in college, and now the subject matter hit much closer to home than she'd ever imagined it would. The book was life-changing to Dianne, in that it gave her encouragement to do what her gut was telling her anyway: "Elisabeth gave me permission to be with Austin and to live. She gave me permission to do what I inherently wanted to do, which was to push back the furniture, put on music, and dance with my child in my arms."

Everyone else, she said, told her to go to every hospital and to fight, fight, fight. But Dianne knew there needed to be more: "Elisabeth gave me a fire in my belly to be a bit more defiant in the face of the medicalization of life."

Dianne's life with Austin is filled with stories of her doing just that. When Austin was about seven she took him and her preschool-aged daughter hiking. As hikers looked at her like she was nuts, Dianne pushed Austin's wheelchair along the rugged nature path, with her daughter perched at its base. They made it to the top of a locally beloved waterfall, where they watched as teenagers gleefully slid down the falls like it was a waterslide. Dianne was struck by memories of doing it herself as a kid and the knowledge that Austin would never get the chance to. "That moment was all we were going to get," Dianne said, "so I adapted." She asked her daughter to stay put on one side of the falls while a friend watched over her. Then she picked Austin up out of his wheelchair and carried him sideways across the top of the falls, stopping to dip his toes while she said, "Ohhh, it's cold! We're going through the waterfall!" Then she set him down safely and went back across to do the same thing with her daughter. "That's what parenting is," Dianne said. "We create magical moments for our kids."

After Austin had been bedridden for three years Dianne wanted him to experience the sensation of swimming again, of being weightless. On a hot day Dianne suggested to the nurse on duty that they get some extra oxygen tubing (Austin used oxygen for comfort care, to help him breathe more easily) and jerry-rig it so he could go outside and get in the pool. The nurse was horrified. "She told me, 'You can't do that. You're going to kill him.'"

Dianne listened to the nurse and didn't do anything just then. "But I could hear what Elisabeth was saying in my ear: don't be irresponsible, but live. So I thought it through again. Would water get into the oxygen tubing? Would we damage the tubes? And I realized it would be fine. I wanted my son to live. I wanted to pack as much life in as we could. So when the next nurse came on duty I brought it up again. I said, 'Can we do this?' And she said, 'Let's do it!'"

The two of them played MacGyver for a bit, then Dianne carried Austin down the steps to the pool. Though he wasn't able to speak, Dianne said, "You could hear him go 'ahhh' because he was floating, because he was free. I had given him a gift."

Through all the years—and there ended up being about nine between Austin's diagnosis and his death—Dianne prayed for one thing. It was not that he would live, because she knew that he wouldn't, that he couldn't with this disease. But she wanted him to go on his own—she did not want to be the person responsible for withholding nutrition and hydration.

And yet that's exactly what happened. Austin was injured one day when a nurse turned him over. He was nonverbal, and yet he was screaming, crying. They couldn't find the source of the pain.

Dianne called the top researcher in the field and said, "What do I do?" But no one had any answers, and his pain continued.

Dianne called for an ethics counsel through her church to advise her because at that time the hospice providing care for Austin didn't have its own ethics committee. She didn't want her friends on it or anyone who would be supportive of Dianne the person—she wanted to be grilled. Her church brought in some of the community, staff, and a few people Dianne knew for a panel. The net-net at the end of the day was that whatever she decided to do, they would support her. "I understood this was on me, and whatever I did I was going to have to live with it.

"When we did it," Dianne said of withholding nutrition, "there was enormous guilt, and there was shame. The first time I went to church after Austin's death I was walking down the aisle and I heard one person say, 'finally.' I walked another twenty feet and heard another person whisper, 'Did you hear she killed her son?'

"And I went and I took communion and I got on my knees and I determined no one would ever understand what it's like to be in my shoes. It was going to be between me and God, and I was going to have to take responsibility for it."

Dianne and her daughter left town for a while after that to travel the world and remember what it was like to be among people again, in a restaurant again, on a plane again. For years Dianne's world had been one of two spaces: outside in nature or in the ten-by-fourteen room where Austin lived.

In her grief, again, Dianne looked to Elisabeth's words. After 9/11 Elisabeth was interviewed by *Time* magazine, and the reporter said something to the effect of, "Isn't this the greatest tragedy ever?" And Elisabeth said, "Have you read about the Holocaust? Have you read about World War II? This is certainly a tragedy—I mean no disrespect. But no, it's not the greatest tragedy." And for Dianne it was the same. "You need to get outside of yourself," she said. "There was a Holocaust. I'm one person who lost one child. Albeit, he was the world to me, but he was one child."

When she returned from her travels Dianne ran into an old acquaintance in a grocery store parking lot who asked her if she was ready to go back to work as a writer. The acquaintance knew of a job with a publisher in the hospice space. Dianne ended up taking the job, and one day a business card from the Elisabeth Kübler-Ross Foundation ended up on her desk. To this day Dianne's not sure how it got there. But she called them to see if they had anything worth writing about, and through an odd sequence of connections, she ended up helping to publish a book called *Tea with Elisabeth*. Her engagement in the foundation deepened when she was asked to join the board, and five years later she was asked to be the president, to be Elisabeth's voice.

"Elisabeth taught me that death is part of life, but it is not all of life. Austin's love still lives on. He is still my son. It manifests for me every day. I was having a conversation yesterday with the man I'm seeing, and I said, 'I have a son. He's not here. And I still need to be cared for as his mom even though my son's physicality is not here. His being is still here, and his spirit is still here.'"

There is no silver lining to be seen in the darkness of a child's death. But there are two learnings. One is that those who have lost a child need people to bear witness. The second goes back to what Greg Lundgren observed, which is that humans can withstand a lot. We are inherently fighters.

"I think we are by far more resilient than we give ourselves credit for," Dianne said. "We can survive things. I didn't die from my pain. I didn't die from my suffering. The brain tells the lungs to breathe, and you breathe. It's horrible, but you're going to live anyway, so what are you going to do with it?"

Next to the death of a child, suicide is arguably the other most difficult death to talk about, and it does in fact seem unspeakable much of the time.

Karen Wyatt is a hospice doctor who you met in Chapter 1. When her father committed suicide, none of her friends knew what to say or do, and Karen, too, retreated into herself when it came to the pain of the loss. "I worried that people would judge my dad who didn't know him. I couldn't bear the pain of him being judged. I worried that someone religious would say, 'He's obviously going to hell.' I didn't approach people for that reason. So I just stayed in a shell for a long, long time with no one to talk to and no one to seek help from. That was intensely painful."

Karen is a writer, though, and she used her writing as a way to process and to heal. Even so, it took her ten years to write directly about her dad's suicide and to then audibly record those stories. Another ten years passed before she offered to share the recordings with her mom.

"My mom said, 'I don't want to talk about it or hear about it,'" Karen said, reminding me again that at the time, twenty years had passed since her dad's death. But the next day her mom said, "I want to hear it. Play one of those stories for me." So Karen played her a recording where she talked about visiting her dad's grave. "We cried and spent that day and the whole night talking about it, talking about his death." For twenty years Karen had assumed her mom and brother blamed her for her father's death because she was a doctor and had dealt with suicidal ideation professionally. "My mom said, 'I assumed you and your brother blamed me.' And my brother said, 'I assumed you and Mom blamed me because I worked with him and was the last person to see him before he died.'"

Karen summed up the silencing effect of suicide in succinct heartbreaking words: "That is the lethal legacy of suicide. We were all carrying our own guilt. Suicide is a different sort of grief because of the depth of guilt that gets attached to it."

It's tragic that we don't talk about suicide, and we don't talk about trauma that often leads to suicide in the first place. The most obvious example of this comes from the military, where the US Department of Veteran's Affairs reported over twenty veteran suicides *a day* in 2016. Studies have shown a clear correlation between PTSD and suicide attempts and suicidal ideation. And what helps with PTSD is talking about trauma.

For twenty years psychologist Joe Ruzek has been working with veterans and specifically focusing on understanding and healing PTSD. He explained the reasons for high rates of PTSD in veterans—reasons that will surprise no one: exposure to one's own risk of death, witnessing harm done to others, survivor guilt, long periods of stress. It's as though our soldiers—and anyone reporting on or spending time in a war zone—encounter an intimacy with death, and then when they come home it's supposed to be scrubbed clean—talk of death needs to stay at arm's length. But that's not the way it works.

"It's interesting," said Joe, "when you think about your dinner conversations about death. Most of the most powerful treatments for PTSD involve open, feeling conversations of a particular kind. Most of them are trauma-focused psychotherapy where people are encouraged to talk about their war-zone experiences in detail while allowing themselves to feel and experience some of the emotions and experiences that they've had. So we think that emotional avoidance of painful memories and the lack of talking about them is part of what maintains this stress and leads to chronic PTSD. In these treatments people are led to express and talk about what happened. By doing that, they become less fearful of their emotional reactions, grow confidence that they can recover, and generate new perspectives on the negative views that they've held."

There are certainly times in life where silence makes sense. For instance, Karen wasn't ready to talk about her dad's suicide right away, and that's understandable—people need to take it at their own pace. But I also feel that the more horrible or un-speakable the death or trauma, the more we need to show we can handle listening. When author and speaker Megan Devine talks about grief, she says that one of the most important things you can do is to "be known as the person who can withstand the details."

If you could extend your life, how many years would you add? Twenty, fifty, one hundred, forever?

As with all these prompts, there is no right answer to how many years you would extend your life, but this question sparks some serious debates and discussion. Some of my favorite responses:

"I'd extend by twenty years. Feels like some parts would rust out by fifty years beyond. Twenty extra might help ensure you can tackle a fraction of the bucket list."

"I do not personally think that my happiness or joy stems from the finite, nor do I think I'm infinite as is (no shame on those who do). So I'd love several centuries to go deeper, and then I'd like, someday, to feel complete and end."

"Assuming good quality of life—long enough to have a meaningful relationship with potential grandchildren—then maybe an extra twenty."

"I already suspect I'm going to live past one hundred, and I don't really want to. I think I'm going to outlive everyone, which seems like a lonely prospect."

"The simplest answer is that I desire to live as long as it is still a verb."

"I'd love to live till the day I can no longer hold a grandbaby, remember my kids' names, drive, feed myself, and walk without assistance AND the day after I lose my last great friend. I have seen how lonely it is to be the only one left over. If that was fifty years, that would be great. And . . . the other side to that question is that I am not sure I want to live in a world with out-of-control climate change. I feel I would yearn too strongly for the days when we had the natural beauty that the world intended us to live in."

And then there's Joon Yun, who has no intention or desire to live forever but would like life to be extended and would like to see if aging can be "cured." For a long time his interest was mainly academic. Joon wondered: *Can senescence—the process of aging—be modified?* The scientific community's answer to that question has always been a firm "no." But Joon came to realize it's not actually provable either way. "You can't prove or disprove senescence is a selectable trait, that it's a code," he said. By "selectable," he means that you can identify it and, in theory, adjust it. "So," he figured, "I'm just going to assume it is selectable, because if it is, the upside is so large." He is a physician turned hedge-fund manager turned founder of the Palo Alto Longevity Prize, a competition designed to—at least on the surface—defeat aging.

Then Joon's father-in-law died, and his interest in aging from a biological perspective crossed over into the realm of the heart. Joon was very close to his wife's father and said, "The hole he left in my heart was far bigger than I ever estimated." His father-in-law had died from a cardiac event related to aging.

As Joon reflected on the loss of intimacy he experienced with his father-in-law's passing, he considered the evolutionary biology of loss. He argues that we weren't evolutionarily wired to experience loss like we do. We were wired to live in small, intimate kin tribes. But that's not what life and relationships look like anymore. We have deeper connections with a wider group of people, and if you look at those relationships as living entities, the death of a person is also the death of all those relationships and networks.

"My father-in-law's death was the catalyst for me to say, 'This is really painful,'" said Joon, "and this is the experience of everybody around the globe. So what can I do to help elongate the shared experience so we can have a more full arc together, not only of our own lives but on the relationship front?"

Joon's goal is to improve what's called "*homeostatic capacity.*" One way he suggests thinking about this type of bioresilience is to envision the ever-popular Weeble toy. When we are young our body is proficient at recentering itself. He characterizes aging as the progressive loss of homeostatic capacity of every function of our body. What if this loss can be prevented or even reversed? So imagine that a fifty-year-old, instead of experiencing creaky knees every time he takes a run, might get a little stiffness, but then his body quickly recovers. And not because he's taking daily cortisone shots but because the body is returning itself to "normal"—like the Weeble, it's recentering itself. "What we're talking about is putting healthcare systems back in the body where it started," Joon said.

"That also makes the business of healthcare really small, delivers a lot more value, and helps people be healthier a whole lot longer. What we're talking about," he emphasized, "is a radical departure from the current system."

In Joon's worldview there will always be 100 percent mortality, but we'll die of the ailments people used to die of before they were able to reach old age, what he calls the "slings and arrows of life" (things like infection and trauma). What he is trying to do is not the knightly quest of defying death but of extending our expectations of a good, healthy, functional life so we can have more time together that isn't clouded by decline. The greatest modern effort for immortality, therefore, is not about immortality at all—it's about life.

"The summer before I lost Kimberly's dad," he said, "the whole family was together sitting around a fire on the Connecticut shore. And I have a distinct memory of that summer. The kids were young; all the parents were still with us. And it occurred to me: I'm living in a precious zone in my life. I was in my forties, and the narrative was that the forties are when you're supposed to have your midlife crisis. But instead I was experiencing an awareness that the people I love most—the children—were in the bosom of the family, and the people who loved me most and the people who loved my wife the most—the grandparents— were still with us. That it's the midlife sweet spot. That it will never be as good as this."

Although much of Joon's focus is on the question *How can we do this?*, there are endless debates on the question of *Should we?*

"Consciously or not, we realize that life without an end would become a flat, featureless expanse, just one thing after another, literally ad infinitum. Endlessness would suck the vitality out of our existence. It would leave us with that sense of tedium and pointlessness that is the hallmark of chronic depression. So the last thing I would ever want is to never die." At seventy-one, Lesley Hazleton held a TED audience rapt with her elegant and sometimes brutal charm. Her talk had sprung from a cocktail conversation with an ardent fan of the end-to-aging movement.

Clearly, the fellow at the cocktail party didn't know who he was tangling with. For five decades Lesley has been delving into questions of immortality, the afterlife, faith, religion, and the biggest questions we face. She has a brain like a surgeon's knife and a poetic flair for words that brings to mind Graham Greene or Virginia Woolf. "He was about half my age," Lesley said of her conversation partner. "And since death was clearly more of an imminent reality for me than for him, he made the mistake of assuming that I would be in mortal fear of it. He seemed quite shocked that I wasn't. In fact, he seemed to take my equanimity at the prospect as an admission of some kind of failure on my part."

As she tells it, she surprised herself and her new young friend when she asked the question: "What is wrong with dying?"

It is a question that is shocking in its simplicity and mind numbing in its utter clarity. What it robs us of is basic assumptions we so often take for granted: night is dark and death is bad.

But perhaps—and just perhaps—death is a gift, or at the very least a defining characteristic of being human. Lesley powerfully hammers this idea home: "We need endings. Because the most basic ending of all is built into us. My mortality does not negate meaning. It creates meaning. It is not how long I live that matters. It is how I live. And I intend to do it well, to the end. We are finite beings within infinity."

Neil deGrasse Tyson, the popular and critically acclaimed author and astrophysicist, famously gave an interview with Larry King where he says that knowing that his time is limited is what drives him: "It is the knowledge that I'm going to die that creates the focus that I bring to being alive. The urgency of accomplishment, the need to express love *now*, not later. If we live forever, why ever even get out of bed in the morning? Because you always have tomorrow. That's not the kind of life I want to lead."

Jason Silva has been commentating on life extension for a decade and is the greatest cheerleader I know for more scientific breakthroughs. He hosts the TV show *Brain Games* and is known for his YouTube series "Shots of Awe," where he passionately considers the oldest philosophical questions we face. Talking to him is also a bit like watching a cyclone.

He had no qualms whatsoever about extending his life. "If we developed radical life-extension technology," he said, "that was able to extend our health span not just our life span—biotechnology, intervention, molecular scale repair, escape velocity—which means we can repair ourselves faster than we can decay, any of those approaches, proven that it's safe enough, I would sign up with no reservations whatsoever. In fact, I think it's the moral imperative for human beings to figure out how to transcend this mortality/death thing."

I wanted to know more as to why he saw it as a moral imperative to transcend death. "It's an unbearable weight on our shoulders of being mortal beings who dream of immortality," he explained. "To be gods and worms at the same time—to be gifted with a self-referential consciousness that can contemplate infinity. Death has become an imposition on the human race and is no longer acceptable. I love deeply. I love family, friends, music, art, cognition, sentience, poetry. I love wonder, I love awe, and I find the concept of being robbed of all of that as intolerable and unacceptable. I think anxiety increases with intelligence, and it becomes increasingly difficult to explain death away."

Jason and I have different perspectives here. If life extension were ever to become possible, I worry about the impact on a planet whose resources are already overtaxed. I worry about the even greater divide we'd see between the rich and the poor. We cannot look at one piece of the puzzle without looking at how it affects the greater whole. I worry, too, about what we lose when we don't face our mortality as a given. I asked him, "Do you not think there's a value in coming to terms with impermanence?"

"I don't mean to sound unsympathetic to people who have found some kind of peace through acquiescence or acceptance of death," he said. "I think if they're at peace, then good for them. Just like people who have belief in God and the afterlife, they probably sleep better at night. I'm not saying that's not a good opiate. Perhaps it's the only opiate in the end if we want to live a tranquil life, but it just doesn't do it for me—I ask too many questions . . ."

Peter Thiel, the cofounder of PayPal, said, "If people think they are going to die, it is demotivating. The idea of immortality is motivational." Lesley Hazelton takes him on: "As one of the people absurd enough to imagine she is going to die," she said, "I find Thiel's glibness astonishing. He reduces existence to the language of corporate management, to motivational pap. He seems to think our lives are invalidated by the fact that we will die. And he assumes that life is a matter of metrics, its value determined by something as easy to calculate as years. In Thiel's world what gets us up in the world is not the joy of the life we are actually living but the hope that we will go on getting up in the morning forever. I for one can think of few things more depressing. Thiel's dream is my nightmare."

I obviously grapple with our cultural avoidance of the topic of death. And I want to make a distinction: this book's inquiry is primarily why we don't discuss our mortality. I completely accept that humans fear death. I think it is very natural for us to be afraid of death—instinctively, philosophically, biologically. At the most basic level we are biological creatures focused on extending our gene line and maintaining our heartbeat.

Many years ago Michael Pollan's book *A Botany of Desire* changed my entire worldview of how and why we, as humans—and most other plants and animals—are hardwired with the mission to continue our DNA through seed or progeny or some division of our cells. In *Botany* Pollan deftly takes us on a first-person journey into the natural world, illustrating the remarkable work at play as the seeds of four plants exert their desire to be reproduced and propagated across as much terrain as possible. He shows us the perspective of the seed. Instead of thinking about the human desire to plant seeds and grow fruit, he flips the equation and shows how humans are—for lack of a better word—manipulated by these intelligently designed plants. He hauntingly and painstakingly shows us humans doing the bidding of the biological DNA in apples, marijuana, potatoes, and tulips. After reading this masterpiece you can no longer look at fruit without an incredible new respect for the intelligence in the system.

I think that our desire for immortality is less about wanting to fish the same perfect fishing hole for millennia and more about the fact that we have these seeds inside of us that have coded instructions to reproduce, continue on, propagate. Think of R2-D2 in *Star Wars*, the droid coded with a distress message from Princess Leia intended for Obi Wan Kenobi. He went to great peril to deliver the message. Essentially, we are both the apple and Johnny Appleseed, R2-D2 and Leia, and it is confusing as hell. We are conscious enough to know that the fruit of the apple—us—will perish, even if our DNA will continue in our offspring.

Ernest Becker, in his 1977 Pulitzer Prize–winning book *The Denial of Death,* makes it a little less pretty: "Man is literally split in two: he has an awareness of his own splendid uniqueness in that he sticks out of nature with a towering majesty, and yet he goes back into the ground a few feet in order to blindly and dumbly rot and disappear forever."

My thinking is that our DNA, not our ego, undoubtedly wants to continue, and we just get the two confused—and this is where I again diverge from Silva and Thiel's view. Ours is not a culture that allows the ego to gracefully sunset after it has done its important work. The ego is a great delivery device, making sure that we preserve ourselves in order to get our basic biological imperative accomplished. It is no wonder that many egos soften as we grow beyond our prime. To vastly oversimplify: in a healthy traditional village, elders think about the community first, young men think about themselves, and women think about their offspring. Many men get terrified when their libido begins to lessen, as their value is wrapped up in their ability to continue their DNA. For evidence, look no further than the rapidly growing erectile dysfunction market, anticipated to be worth more than $3.2 billion by 2022.[1] Women also endure great stress as their biological clocks begin to reach their terminus.

Regardless of how we try to hide it or obscure it, we are biological beings. A flower might be wise to choose to not burst forth in blossom, deciding to preserve its energy. Flowering begins the almost immediate death of a flower, yet it has no choice. Life is designed to be lived. Contrast that with humans, as we are not necessarily all allowing ourselves full bloom, and Becker reminds us that "guilt results from unused life, from the unlived in us."

To sum up this deep dive into life extension and primal fear: I hope that we can begin to be more clear: Are we afraid of talking about death, or are we afraid of dying? Are we afraid of dying, or are we afraid of not having left an authentic mark on the world? And perhaps we can shed even more of our presumptions and anxiety and accept that it is enough to just have lived and then died. As Lesley so poignantly asked: What's wrong with dying?

What do you want your legacy to be?

I've heard many different answers to the question of what you want your legacy to be, and for most people who have children, that is where the conversation starts and ends. But I particularly love it when the conversation goes far beyond the obvious.

"Why doesn't someone set up a trust and pay an ice cream shop to give a free ice cream cone away every Friday?" Greg Lundgren suggested. He's been known to think expansively about the question of legacy and has often thought of writing a book listing unconventional ways to leave a mark on the world. "Or arrange for a flower shop to give away a red rose on a certain day of the week." Or, he said, perhaps, if your grandmother was a ballerina in her youth, "you could establish a scholarship to send a young dancer to school. When you start thinking of it, the options are many and fit any budget."

Although Tyler's mother, Doree, who I first mentioned on page 74, was not explicit about what she wanted her legacy to be, it was clear to him. She had been a gifted artist, illustrator, art dealer, teacher, and collector. She died of breast cancer when Tyler was twenty-seven, and all her artwork—completed and not—and her vast art collection passed to him. So did her incredible love for art. Tyler is an artist too, though he's quick to say that he's nowhere close to being as talented as his mother. He works as an art director for a major publisher where he collaborates with talented individuals, from wunderkind designers and software engineers to world-class authors and illustrators. The language he uses in his work to explain why something works or doesn't, he said, all came from what his mother taught him. "She was a lifelong teacher, and I think what she appreciated the most about her life was her ability to give people the ability to understand art and the awakening you get from understanding the creative process. Her biggest talent was explaining art in a way that everyone could understand. She could talk to someone who was completely opposed to contemporary art, who would say, 'I don't get it. My preschooler could make this.' Her ideal conversation was to turn them around and get them to appreciate the thought behind the work."

Her art collection has taken years to sift through, as Tyler contemplates the meaning of each piece. "I feel like I'm going to be sorting through their lives for the rest of my life," he said of the inheritance of his mother and stepfather.

"I think a lot about where I fit in, in all of this," he said. "Where they end and I start. I feel like I have strong opinions about my life and where I want it to go and what I want to keep around myself. But I'm also aware that my life is a culmination of everything that came before me."

When I asked the legacy question at a dinner I hosted, I saw a light and what looked like a sharp pain spark in Sandy's thoughtful eyes. I waited to see if she would tell us about Nigeria. I knew the story intimately, but it isn't the kind of story you coax out of someone. She sat and listened attentively as, one at a time, those around the table answered the question. Many of those present were parents who talked about living on through their children. Sandy was not a parent, though she was a devoted aunt to a few and beloved mentor to many. She had also been in the unique position of thinking about her legacy at a moment of near death, and when it came to her turn to speak, as I hoped she would, she told the story.

A filmmaker, Sandy Cioffi was in Nigeria on her fourth trip to capture final interviews for her award-winning documentary

Sweet Crude when the Nigerian military took her team into custody. "The young boys who apprehended us were just as terrified as we were," she said. They loaded the crew into a van to take them to an undisclosed location. In the van Sandy and her crew asked if they could play music on their iPods. Their desire to do so was strategic: they wanted to run the batteries down so their captors wouldn't be able to search their data.

It was one of many eleventh-hour gears that started turning in Sandy's remarkably clear head as the group was moved from a military location, where they were detained by members of the local military and taken by gunpoint back to their hotel and then to a series of less official bunkers, with less official criminals holding them captive. The writing was on the wall: they had been sold to a militant group, and the likelihood of their release had dimmed. Among her team was a Nigerian community leader named Joel, and he gravely confirmed what Sandy was beginning to fear: short of some kind of miracle, they were likely going to be assassinated, but not until after they had been used for ransom and a false story.

Mercifully, most of us never have to look a death sentence in the eye. Standing at the ledge of the sharp cliff of death created immediate lucidity for Sandy. It dawned on her that her death would be blamed on the very resistance movement they were there to champion and defend.

In a miraculous moment of cell connection, Sandy's team had been able to send a couple of texts before their phones were confiscated. One SOS made its way to an aide of Senator Maria Cantwell, and one was to a crew member, Cliff. The text to Cliff said one simple word: "Tiananmen." He immediately knew what that meant and began to destroy any nonessential footage and all maps and contact lists. He stuffed as much data as possible onto four memory sticks, which he taped behind the toilet in the hotel bathroom. This was the same method used by the photographer who captured the famous pictures of the Tiananmen Square riot—it was the only reason the West saw the footage of that fateful day in China.

Back in the bunker, unaware that the text messages had landed, Sandy's thoughts kept going back to the rebels and freedom fighters she had befriended over years of working in the country. This labyrinthine network was engaged in a bloody war with the Nigerian state. The state was backed by Chevron and other multinational oil companies that had been sucking the delta dry of oil for decades, destroying the lands and waters that these farmers and fishermen called home. Sandy felt her Northern white privilege like a guilty weight, her social justice ambitions like an albatross in her throat. Would all her efforts of the past many years be lost to a headline? Sandy was overcome by the icy fear that their captivity and death would ignite a merciless genocide of the community of farmers and fishermen who had taken her in like family and bravely shared their stories. To see your death causing a domino of other deaths is unimaginable. Very few human beings will ever find themselves in this predicament, and despite hours spent as a child with the nuns at St. Patrick's in Brooklyn, Sandy didn't believe in a benevolent God waiting to greet her or know what would happen to her when she died. But she did have a clear sense of what she wanted to leave behind.

During the hours of interrogation and being asked to make false statements on video about her film and the work she had been doing for the past five years in Nigeria, Sandy had fixated on her three-year-old nephew. She knew that the false narrative would likely become one of the ways her nephew Adam would come to know Aunt Sandy, her work, and what her life stood for. She faced her captors squarely and maintained the integrity behind their mission in Nigeria.

Hours after the fateful text was sent out, US Senator Maria Cantwell was woken up in the middle of the night. Despite the hour, she kicked into high gear. Her team had to convince the State Department that they were operating on good intel, that US citizens were in a life-or-death situation in Lagos, Nigeria, and that every second counted. It is very difficult to move a case to highest priority, and luckily the wind was at the film crew's back.

In the dank bunker Sandy's phone began ringing in one of the guard's pockets. The men guarding them looked at the head captor, and he, much to everyone's surprise, handed the phone to Sandy. It was a representative from the US consulate. She asked Sandy several simple questions about her physical state and whereabouts and then asked to talk to who was in charge. Sandy handed the phone to the guard; he listened, snorted, ended the call, and barked a few orders to his men. Within minutes they were gone.

Thirty minutes later a Nigerian military squad entered the bunker and took them back to a military prison in Abuja. Before they were returned to US custody the head of the Nigerian Intelligence summoned Sandy to his office, and as he leaned back in his chair, chewing on a cigar, he laughed, "Who are you? You must be very famous in America." She just stared, bewildered by his lighthearted candor. He continued to laugh and detailed the political currency it took to find her in time and return her to US custody, clearly amazed that she had made it out of his corrupt country alive. Back home Sandy's story had become headline news. A week later she sent a Nigerian friend into the hotel room to recover the files so the movie could be finished. Her efforts were the final push to pass a Senate bill that demands transparency for multinational companies' spending in conflict countries so that we can now see if corporations are arming militias or committing other egregious acts.

As Sandy finished this story, the candles were just nubs, and the wine had dwindled down to the dregs. Everyone was quiet for a moment, processing her words. There are many things to glean from Sandy's story, and we were all grappling with them. Among them was the clarity that she received at death's edge and her desire to leave behind a memory of a life lived along a larger selfless path, truly echoing Stewart Brand's credo, "My client is Civilization." There was also her acute awareness of the next generation and a desire to leave them a message about honesty and tenacity, tracks in the snow that they could follow if they felt the call.

From the time Bud was a young boy growing up in the woodlands of Illinois, he collected found historical objects. A field would be tilled, and treasures would find their way to Bud's collection. A lifelong love of archeology was born. Bud never stopped collecting, through years as a park ranger and then owner of an antique shop. By the time of his death his collection included opium bottles, woven baskets, pottery, African beads, fishing memorabilia, parks memorabilia, and vintage decoy ducks.

Emily didn't meet Bud until she was in college. Bud and his wife, Evelyn, were close friends with Emily's grandmother, who insisted that Emily come meet them. Emily was studying archeology, and her grandma knew how much she would appreciate Bud's hobby.

On their first meeting Bud led Emily into a room filled wall to wall with antique curio cabinets and shelves holding his vast collection. "It was like an open storage archeology museum," Emily said admiringly. Bud had applied a cataloguing system to all his pieces, painstakingly documenting the year it came in, its grouping number, and giving it an item number.

Bud took something from a cabinet. "Do you know what this is?" he asked, showing her a greenish stone tool that came to a shallow point.

"Is that a Folsom point?" Emily asked. It was, and Bud was impressed with Emily's knowledge of this evidence of early civilization in North America.

A friendship was quickly formed between the college student and the octogenarian, and he told her he would show her more and more of the collection each time she came back. "The strangest thing he had in there," said Emily, "was a human vertebra with an arrowhead stuck in it that he picked up in the desert somewhere."

When Emily was still in college Bud and Evelyn asked her if she would consider being a trustee of their estate. "I didn't understand what that meant, but I knew it meant a lot to them that I say yes, and so I did," Emily said. She sensed that Bud and Evelyn's family did not share her interest in their collection, and the couple may have worried it would be undervalued when they were gone. Emily didn't think much more about it until recently, when Bud died, just a few years after Evelyn.

I asked Emily why Bud hadn't given his items away during his lifetime, and she posited that it was too special to him to part with, that the items were wrapped up in memories of where and when he'd found them, and that he liked keeping them close. "My gut feeling is that he would want them to be at an institution like an anthropological museum or an educational setting—a university. He'd want them somewhere where they can be cared for and used for learning."

"Collectors," Emily mused, "so often see themselves as stewards."

One of the most shocking pieces of Lucy and Paul Kalanithi's story is Elizabeth Acadia Kalanithi, aka Cady, born only two years before Paul died, a decision the couple made late in his terminal state. As Paul writes so poignantly in *When Breath Becomes Air*, "It had been something we always wanted . . . to add another chair to the family's table." I asked Lucy about making that decision. "We knew it was crazy," she said. "We knew what was going to happen, that the cancer would most likely take him. It obviously required all kinds of family support and buy-in. And tolerance of uncertainty. I don't think anyone decides to have a child because they think it is going to be easy. It's all about accepting uncertainty. Paul was initially way more certain than I was—he even wanted to have twins."

In *Breath Becomes Air* Lucy asks Paul, "Don't you think saying goodbye to your child will make your death more painful?" And Paul responds, "Wouldn't it be great if it did?" He added later, "We would carry on living, instead of dying."

My parents made the decision to have me with full knowledge that the likelihood of my father seeing me graduate from college, let alone high school, was slim. They must have known that this would bring a sadness and hardship into my life. And yet, as Lucy and I discussed, it's often the difficulties that children face that give them the character they need to thrive. "Parents wish they could take away the struggle from their kids' lives, but it's the difficulty that actually enriches us as humans," she said. And I'm living proof of that: my father's death early in my life led quite clearly to some of my most defining characteristics.

Paul had this to say about his future daughter and her life without him: "I hope I'll live long enough that she has some memory of me. Words have a longevity I do not. I had thought I could leave her a series of letters—but what would they really say? I don't know what this girl will be like when she is 15; I don't even know if she'll take to the nickname we've given her. There is perhaps only one thing to say to this infant, who is all future, overlapping briefly with me, whose life, barring the improbable, is all but past.

"That message is simple. When you come to one of the many moments in life when you must give an account of yourself, provide a ledger of what you have been, and done, and meant to the world, do not, I pray, discount that you filled a dying man's days with a sated joy, a joy unknown to me in all my prior years, a joy that does not hunger for more and more, but rests, satisfied. In this time, right now, that is an enormous thing.[1]

Lucy finished Paul's book, which was number one on the *New York Times* nonfiction bestseller list for twelve weeks, stayed on the list for over a year, and thrust Lucy into the spotlight. "Strangers ask me about Paul all of the time. And it is incredibly helpful. If you are grieving, oftentimes the main thing you want to be doing is connecting with people about your loss rather than pretending that things are okay. And the book tour for Paul allowed me to really help establish and continue his legacy, which was very meaningful to me." Paul's legacy lives on in Cady, in the empowered activism that Lucy brings to the world, and in his profoundly vulnerable and honest exploration of what it means to live while dying.

How long should we grieve?

Carla Fernandez was a senior in college when her dad, Jose, was diagnosed with brain cancer. He passed away a year later, and Carla spent the last six months of his life caring for him, just as all her friends were finishing college, going backpacking, and complaining about guys they were dating. There wasn't much about Carla's reality they could relate to.

The traditional grief support groups didn't connect with Carla either. "It felt institutional," Carla said about the group meeting she attended. "It only held space for a certain set of feelings. There was a box of tissues in the center of a circle, fluorescent lighting, no foreplay. It felt anonymous. I left that night and got on a bus to meet friends at a bar. I needed friendship and connection in a space I felt comfortable." And yet she was tired of getting the "deer in the headlights look" from friends who didn't know what to say.

She moved to Los Angeles soon after, and when she was interviewing for a job at *GOOD* magazine, she met someone who had just started working there that day: Lennon Flowers. She recognized a kindred spirit. Both were starting their careers, both had recently moved to Los Angeles, and both were dating musicians. As the two talked, Carla let it slip that her dad had recently died. "I expected silence, but instead she said 'me too.'"

Lennon had lost her mom to cancer when she was a senior in college and felt her story had become too complicated to air with friends. "Any time I brought it up," Lennon told me, "I felt like saying, 'I'm sorry for making you uncomfortable with my life. I promise to never ever do that again.'"

Regardless of what happened with the job at *GOOD* magazine (which, incidentally, Carla was offered), Carla and Lennon decided they should get together and have a dinner where they could dig into their histories more.

Carla knew a few other women who had also experienced loss, and she invited them over with Lennon for a potluck. "There was a bit of tension and awkwardness when people got there, but a half an hour in, I did a toast to my dad and the floodgates opened," she said. "It was the first time many of us could let our questions out."

They talked about their grief and where they were in their journey, but they also talked about some of the more practical aspects. "What happens when you're on a first date," Carla posited, "and someone asks what do your parents do? Do you lie? Do you change the subject? There were a lot of practical questions that none of us had a sounding board for."

By the end of the evening they all acknowledged that what happened that night was special and necessary, and they decided to do it again. They got together once a month for a year. As twenty- and thirtysomethings heard about what Carla and Lennon were doing, they wanted in too. And so the Dinner Party was born, powered by the potential of forming microcommunities of people in their twenties and thirties who have experienced a significant loss.

As Lennon and Carla formalized their organization and began the process of matching people up around the country, they got pushback from people in the more traditional grief support world. After all, neither Lennon nor Carla were trained as therapists; there were no letters before or after their names. "People would say, 'Oh, that sounds dangerous. You're playing with fire,'" said Lennon. "But we instinctively pushed through it. We look back on it and realize we were being told that creating spaces where humans can be humans is wrong. It's crazy that we live in a culture where talking about this is seen as dangerous."

The two women—who have formed an incredibly close bond of friendship—give a lot of thought to ways in which their generation interacts with grief and how their peer group of "share everything" was born from a generation who said don't talk about the hard stuff. Though compulsive sharing has some negative associations, on balance Lennon and Carla think it's not only healthier but also necessary. "We don't have the framework, rituals, or belief systems to make sense of the unknowable," said Carla. "I think that's where a lot of the feeling of being totally unmoored comes from for people. There's nothing for them to hold on to. We're so quick to numb it out and get back to work. But in my belief, grief is this incredible process of metabolization. A praising that people were ever in our lives and a praising of life. Not going there does such a disservice."

Since January 2014 the Dinner Party has grown from a few dozen people to more than four thousand who meet regularly at more than 230 tables in a hundred-plus cities and towns worldwide. Among the great lessons Lennon and Carla have learned in their work growing the organization is that grief doesn't ever completely disappear. Those clamoring to join their tables are often people who have lost someone years and even decades prior. The idea of a timeline, of a beginning and end point to grief, is nonsensical. "As a culture we need to move the conversation from a commonplace understanding of the five phases of grief, to ways that we are perpetually changing but still colored by the absence of that life," said Lennon.

Grief has no time limit, it is not about time. It is about letting go of a person we loved, a future that we imagined them in, and it also means letting go of a part of ourselves that we may be attached to. There is a wound that is created, and every wound heals at a different rate.

That's why the prompt "How long should we grieve?" is a little misleading, though I've found it's a great way to open the conversation. We may look at grief in terms of time, and it's often true that the first year is the hardest and that time does heal—but not always, and not completely. Grief is not like an illness you get over, and there is no "should" in grief. Grief itself looks different throughout the course of a lifetime. Truth be told, it looks different throughout the course of the day.

It's been said that we're not as afraid of death as we are of grief. I think it is worth meditating on that thought. It is pretty immense.

The thing about grief and about losing someone who is incredibly close to us, is that there are two deaths, not just one. We lose a person who we love. They are gone, unfathomably erased from the present, and, more achingly, from the future. As modern humans we love the feel of endless potential; we love the *magic* of life, that the future is a technicolor pattern of endless possibility. When someone dies, we lose a whole ecosystem of possibility. All the future moments, all the future laughter is no longer, and for many of us it feels like a theft. This is the first death, the loss of the person.

The second death—and this is where the math gets a little tricky, so hang in there with me—is the part of us that must also die. It is the part of us that was connected to that person. The closer the connection, the more severe the second death is. One of the core pieces of many age-old rituals is letting a part of us die. A wedding does this—a wedding is a celebration of a union, it is a birth, but it is also a funeral for the *single* you. If you don't let the *single* you die at that altar, I can assure you that the new union will be short-lived. A bar or bat mitzvah does this, as does a walkabout, where you are letting go of a childhood in service to a future of greater learning and service.

Chanel Reynolds, who lost her husband when he was just forty-three, touches on something that comes up again and again with those who have lost someone close to them: you're not just mourning the person who died; you're also mourning the person you were when they were alive. "People will ask me, especially people who are new on this path, they plead with me, 'It gets better, right?'" she said. "I say, 'Absolutely, sweetie. But it gets different.'" Chanel is different now from who she was before her husband's fatal bike accident. Lennon and Carla are different from who they were when their parents were alive.

This idea has many ripples, so it's not just about the person in grief but about everyone around them. When you are not the same as you were, it can be difficult to engage with other people in your life in the same way. Dianne Gray, who you may recall lost her son and now heads up the Elisabeth Kübler-Ross Foundation, talks to people in grief about this all the time. People will say to her, "My mom doesn't understand how to be there for me. My best friend isn't reaching out to me. My friends left me." And Dianne tells them, not unkindly, "'That's the way it goes, sister, because people are people. In times of grief, choose your tribe.'" Dianne acknowledges that it causes people distress when she says it, but that doesn't mean it's not true. "I explain, you're not the same person anymore. And it's important to validate that loss and give space for it. You have to mourn your loss of identity. And if you're not the same person, don't you think your friends are going to have a difficult time adjusting?"

"To a person," Dianne said, "what they say back is 'People should love me for who I am.'"

Another way of saying this is that people should be loyal. But loyalty is in and of itself a judgment. "Some people simply cannot be with a dying child," Dianne said. "They cannot be with a grieving person." The nonjudgment that Elisabeth Kübler-Ross embodied so powerfully, Dianne explained, means allowing people to be where they are. And for those in grief to focus on who *can* be there for them, to focus the same time it would take to focus on the negative forces in their lives instead focusing on the positive. And to leave space for the unknown, as Lennon and Carla did, because you never know what—or who—will enter. You might just find each other.

~

While Lennon and Carla described many of their generation as unmoored and dinners as a way to bring connection in grief, religious traditions have been doing this since ancient times, offering guardrails to hold us in the emotional chaos.

Sharon Brous has frequently been named one of the United States's most influential rabbis. I attribute this to many of her gifts, but foremost among them is her clarity of thinking. When we talked about ritual and its importance in the Jewish tradition, then, it seemed strange that she would start by telling me a story about her husband starting his MFA program in film at the same time she started rabbinical school. But as usual, the connection was spot on.

Sharon's husband, David, was at his first day of film school in New York. The professor handed out video cameras, split the students into groups of four, and sent them out into the city with the instruction: "You have eight hours to create a three- to five-minute film." "David said it was the most frustrating experience,"

Sharon explained. "Here he is, finally in film school, everyone's so excited and animated around the idea, but all they did was argue the whole day."What they came up with was terrible, and the same was true for every group. David was completely bummed out.

The next day the professor sent the groups out again to make a three- to five-minute film in eight hours, but this time he gave them more instruction. In the film they were to make, there was the loosest plot imaginable: "A" needs to give something to "B." "B" rejects what "A" is offering. And "A" reacts.

This time what they came back with was surprising, beautiful. It was art.

"I thought, 'That's what ritual is,'" Sharon said. "That's what ritual does for us as Jews. This whole world is beautiful, but it's almost too vast and you don't know how to hold it. But if a container is held around the experience, you have a chance to make art."

Right after someone dies in the Jewish faith, the focus is on burial of the body as soon as possible. "There is a forceful immediacy to that experience," Sharon said. "It gives people something to do when you have no idea what to do right now. Everything you knew to be true is gone. And instead of throwing your hands up and saying, 'I don't know what to do,' the tradition says, 'Here's what you do.'"

Jewish ritual also forces a confrontation with a new reality. Most notably, the family has the job of covering the coffin with earth. "That might seem unforgiving," Sharon said, "but people talk about the sound of earth hitting the top of a wooden coffin as the most important moment for them in starting the grieving process. There's something so visceral about it. It pushes us toward the confrontation of truth, which is that this person isn't in the world as she was before."

The ritual continues with sitting shiva, in which the family goes home and stays there for seven days while people come to them. Like with burial, the tradition is carefully prescribed. Visitors bring food. They wait to speak until the family speaks so that the family can set the tone. In this way shiva gives an answer to that most unhelpful of questions: What can I do to help? Shiva tells you: You show up. You bring food. You wait for them to speak, and then you follow their lead.

"There's wisdom to the tradition of giving you space to cry and to share stories and to laugh and to be surrounded by love and by food for seven days when you otherwise might forget to eat, forget to laugh, and not know how to cry, and not want to bother people by telling your stories," Sharon said. "It's built to create a container for grief which might not grow so easily. And it's a lot. It's hard to sit for seven days and do this. Some people feel they're done after three, but I think there's something about the relentlessness of it that pushes people to the reality of loss and the necessity of grief."

On the last of the seven days you get up with whoever is there, and you walk together around the block. You can be silent, or you can sing. As Sharon explained it, it's a way of saying that your loved one died, but you're still alive. People out in the world are going to work and to school. You haven't seen these signs of life going on in the past seven days, nor should you have had to. But now you can. It's a gentle re-entry into the land of the living.

The next phase of mourning is the repeated recitation of the Kaddish, the mourner's prayer for the dead, in a group. "It's not that those words are an expression of what the mourner is feeling," said Sharon. "They're usually not. I've come to understand that it's not about the words; again, it's about creating a container to hold grief. And that container is the same one the person across the room is holding, which is the same as my great-grandparents held. And when you say those words—*Yitgadal v'yitkadash shmei Rabbah*—the whole community responds *AMEN!,* which is their way of saying, 'I see you. I can't take your pain away, but I can help hold you.'"

"The notion is that of community," said Rabbi Amichai Lau-Lavie, a rabbi in New York who has faced some remarkable challenges in his still-young career, including being an openly gay religious leader despite the fact that he hails from a spiritual power family. (His uncle was the chief rabbi of Israel.) When Amichai's father passed away three years ago Amichai flew to Israel for his funeral and remained with his mother in Jerusalem for the next month. Many people back home wanted to be with him as he said Kaddish, and because he was far away, he had the idea to have a phone call. "At a certain moment people dialed in, and I said a few words, and we said Kaddish. Then I did the same thing the following week."

It's powerful to say Kaddish as a group—in fact, tradition dictates it should be minyans of ten—and the fact that it happened via telephone didn't change that. So he suggested people call in every Thursday at 3 P.M. and that they keep it going. They have been doing it regularly for three years. "Sometimes people just say their name," he said. "Sometimes we share poetry. Then we say Kaddish, and the whole thing takes maybe twenty or thirty minutes." The numbers on the call range from five to fifty, sometimes more. "I don't insist that it's ten people," he said. "Or that it's Jews. We're inviting people who are grieving to not be alone. To just be together to connect to something bigger, to channel grief into this contemplative moment." Amichai has received constant pushback from the orthodox community, as it is never popular to adjust a tradition as old as Kaddish, but it has sparked new passion for ritual in many who had left Judaism entirely.

Islamic rituals surrounding death are, at the core, very simple. Hisham Farajallah, who is on the board of trustees at the Idriss Mosque in Seattle, explains that when a Muslim dies, the body is cleaned and shrouded with cloth. The cloth represents protection, but its simplicity is also symbolic: "We're born with nothing," Hisham said, "and we leave with nothing." The body is prayed over and laid in a small house—not a box, per se—and the face of the deceased is turned toward Mecca. All of this happens in very short order, as in Islam, you want to bury the body as soon as possible—on the same day of the death if it can be managed. Condolences will be offered either at the graveside or at the home of the deceased. And for three days people cook for the deceased's family. Beyond that, Hisham said, it's very personal, and an individual can choose what grieving process feels right for them. He said that after his father died, people came for weeks and months, which was welcomed but not required. And many people will give to charity on behalf of the person who has died and include them in their daily prayers.

While the process Hisham described is universal, Muslims live all over the world, and Islamic culture varies dramatically from place to place. Amanda Saab, for instance, grew up in a Muslim culture where rituals surrounding grief go on for much longer. Amanda was the first major reality TV contestant to wear a hijab, and this controversial headscarf sparked a stream of hate mail and even death threats. Her response was to invite strangers into her home, and she began a dinner series called *Dinner with Your Muslim Neighbor*. Her immensely courageous gamble was that if people knew more about what it means to be Muslim, there would be less hate and brutality focused on Muslims, the majority of whom are focused on peace.

At one of her dinners Amanda taught me about the rituals she grew up with surrounding death. Generally, she said, everyone gathers at the mosque before the graveside ceremony, and the family of the deceased sits at a table next to the casket—women on one side, men on the other—and people clad all in black line up to offer condolences. It's an emotional, somber day, and after the burial the community provides a meal.

In the days that follow, as Hisham explained, the family home of the deceased is filled with visitors. "They're constantly being supported," said Amanda, "and being fed, and having the opportunity to talk about the loved one who died." And much like shiva, food is a central piece—required for three days, but often continuing long after that. "When you think about food and nourishment, it's what gives us life. And here we're talking about food and the end of life. It's an interesting paradox. It's so important around death, in that people in the grieving process aren't able to care for themselves and think about nourishing themselves. So to have people bringing food to sustain life after someone has died is pretty powerful.

"After a week," Amanda continued, "there's what's called a spouh." It's another gathering at the mosque, wherein the family again sits at the head at long tables, and everyone offers condolences. There is prayer, usually a eulogy and speeches, and then another meal. After forty days, Amanda explained, there is another spouh. And then another on the one-year anniversary of the loved one's death. Then, after a year or two, the family hosts a community gathering in their loved one's honor. This time they sponsor the meal to share with everyone, and though it's more lighthearted, there are still tears and space for grief.

What's particularly notable to me about this process is how well it honors the grieving process. Grief feels differently in the days following death than it does a week and then a month later. But it is still there. It is still there at a year. It is still there at two years. Yet as time passes, there is room to be more celebratory.

While little is expected of the mourning family in the aftermath of their loss and they are essentially propped up by their community, when they are a couple of years out, they are better able to honor their loved one with energy they never could have mustered in the days after the death and to thank their community for being there for them.

I asked Amanda if she thought all the public mourning was ever too much. After all, I can't imagine, in the days after a loss, wanting to be surrounded by people constantly, let alone sitting at a table and having to talk to a long line of mourners. Where is the room for private grief? "I've definitely felt that it can be too much," Amanda said. "What if you want to be by yourself, cry alone, not be surrounded by all these people? What if you are having to spend all this energy you don't have trying to be respectful to people who visit? There have been times when I've felt family members did not want it. They kept their head down, hand out, but were not really engaged. But I think the culture overpowers their personal preference." Even so, Amanda thought that community may have significance that the mourner cannot see. "Maybe as you're grieving you don't see how important having support and not being alone could be to you, but you come to appreciate it later."

When Cora suddenly lost her brother when he was just forty-two, her primary feeling was that she wanted to join him. Her grief was so strong that even her husband and children could not rouse her from it. The intensity of her grief frightened people—those who loved her worried for her mental health. "Our culture has nowhere to put these dark feelings and sorrow," she wrote.

"The saying that kept me afloat on some of my hardest days was 'The depth of your grief is equal to the depth of your love.' That is exactly how it felt." It's a feeling other cultures know well and accept. She pointed out that in Middle Eastern cultures, common words of solace are "Don't die with the dead," which implies that of course you want to die with your loved one, but please stay.

Cora wants other people to know just how very dark it gets—and that it is okay. In a moving piece for the *Huffington Post* she wrote, "Your pain is normal, socially accepted and even embraced in cultures less frightened than ours. . . . When you tell me you just want to die, I for one will not be alarmed, but will say instead, 'I know. Of course you do.'"[1]

We try to pull people out of grief because it scares us and because it's hard to bear witness to. We're fixers. We're doers. But there is no fixing death or the feelings that come from deep grief.

Rabbi Susan Goldberg—or, simply, "Rabbi Susan"—is a former choreographer and a mother who is a leader of one of the largest synagogues in Southern California. She is also the real-world rabbi that the acclaimed Netflix series *Transparent* built a character around. When I talked with Rabbi Susan about grief, she said that she's learned the most by listening deeply to people experiencing it. Listening to someone also means listening to their body, and her dance background makes her particularly attuned. She is highly aware of how grief affects us physically. "I think people are surprised by how tired they feel. You have to save space to feel fatigue in grief.

"I've also noticed people talk about waves of grief," she said. "I call them ocean waves. It seems to help people to not be surprised by these waves. Grief moves through you. And sometimes you feel like this wave of sadness is never going to end. It's so big;

it's so all encompassing. But it does move through you. It does leave. Then you have breaks in the waves. And then there's guilt. There's a feeling like 'Why am I not in the wave of grief? Should I not be feeling relieved that I'm not overwhelmed?'" She teaches to not judge or hold onto it but just to observe it.

"The other big physical thing is anger," she said. "I always try to talk to as many people in the family as I can so that everyone can be aware that if one or other members of the family gets angry, that that's part of grief. It can come out in things that are silly. They can be angry because they can't find their shoes. Everyone needs to be aware that for the next couple of months it's not about shoes. All of the wires are a little more exposed."

A point I feel is important to make is that although I want us to talk about death and firmly believe that our lives are better when we do, talking about death does not make grief any better. Megan Devine, who writes and speaks about grief, spoke eloquently about this tension. "Accepting that death happens does not make it okay," she said. She talked about hearing from people in grief who feel that the "death positive" movement—which is the belief that engaging with death is healthy and natural—can sometimes feel more hip than helpful. "There is a chasm," she said, "between the way we talk about death and the way we live with grief."

"Accepting death doesn't mean you won't be devastated when someone you love dies," wrote mortician Caitlyn Doughty. "It means you will be able to focus on your grief, unburdened by bigger existential questions like 'Why do people die?' and 'Why is this happening to me?' Death isn't happening to you. Death is happening to us all."[2]

Losing a loved one is not something that you ever, ever need to get over. But it is my great hope that we can carry them with us in a way that moves our lives forward.

What would you eat for your last meal?

In the United States the death penalty is legal in thirty-two states. Regardless of where you land on this controversial set of laws, the fact remains that most death-row inmates are able to request their wishes for their final meal. In our penal system, not known for its tenderness, this gesture glimmers, acknowledging, at least in some concessional capacity, the inmate as human.

I couldn't help researching a few death-row last meals. In his "No Seconds" series, photographer Henry Hargreaves captures the haunting images of death-row inmates' last meal requests. He had long been fascinated by food, having worked as a bartender in a restaurant. He told CBS of his bartending days: "The way that people ordered and interacted with their food, and, you know, modified it and treated it . . . I felt like you could pretty much stereotype who they were without even really talking to them, just from their orders."

Victor Feguer was put to death in Iowa by hanging at the age of twenty-eight. For his last meal Feguer requested a single olive with the pit in it. Of all his "No Seconds" photos, Hargreaves says this is his favorite.

"It's just such a polarizing image. We think about last meals, and is it something that's going to be totally gluttonous? And then he just has a single olive," Hargreaves told CBS. "You know, it's so simple, beautiful, and kind of final. It's like a full stop at the end of his life."

Asking our loved ones about their wishes for their final meal does not need to be introduced in terms of death row nor does it even beg the grim reaper into the conversation. Luckily the last meal question is still seen as benign, almost fanciful, like something you'd see on the *New York Times*'s "36 Questions to Fall in Love." It is a safe way to introduce the conversation about end-of-life wishes, final chapter preparation, even without being detected as a #deathconversation.

Though it's a playful question, I agree with Henry Hargreaves that you can learn a lot about a person through their relationship with food. And so I asked a few people who you've already met in this book how they would answer it. I leave the interpretation up to you:

Ira Byock:

Well . . . I'm not sure how hungry I'll be in the hours before my death. However, if I were a political prisoner condemned to die in the morning (undoubtedly for my leftist leanings), I would choose fettuccine carbonara with coconut cream pie for dessert.

Tony Back:

I'd want my last meal to be all about the love and intention from the people who grew the food, cooked it, fed it to me, sat with me while I ate it, and cleaned me up afterwards. Maybe just a radish from someone's backyard garden, on some home-made bread with a smear of butter and a sprinkle of salt. And I'd want this meal to enable us both, even if just for a moment, to experience the love and care and intention we brought to feeding, serving, and loving each other over our lives. All the most important things are those we are given and give away.

Anastasia Higginbotham:

Warm, fresh bread. Lots of butter. And soup—pumpkin or sweet potato or greens, or all three. Black and cayenne pepper. I would be so happy with that. I would be less afraid. A meal like that makes me feel so much love for this life that I can maybe almost be ready to accept my death.

Lucy Kalanithi:

Chocolate-peanut butter pie. It was my favorite dessert as a child, and I have a personal tradition where I'll ALWAYS order chocolate-peanut butter pie if it shows up on a dessert menu anywhere (even if I wasn't planning to have dessert!). So usually I eat this dessert unexpectedly, which makes it even more joyful. Seems right for my last meal to be a—deliberate for once—celebration of that.

Bill Frist:

I'm not sure what I'd actually choose, but as a physician this is precisely what I'd recommend to my patients:

Carrots (to see clearly, especially in the dark)
Coffee (bottomless cup, to capture the sense of
   never-ending eternity)
Spinach (to be strong)
Milk (to bookend your first meal)

I think about my last meal often. And there is one meal that always sticks out in my mind. A chef named Morgan Brownlow used to make me a pasta dish at the end of certain magical nights at our restaurant in Portland, Oregon. The restaurant, clark-lewis, is still open, but the dish is traveling somewhere with this particular mad genius. For a time we were the busiest and arguably most exciting restaurant in the Northwest, and it felt like New York had landed in a grimy industrial section of Stumptown. A well-choreographed night at a restaurant has a quality of perfectly performed ballet—you have left everything on the stage and are filled to the brim with the energy and intoxication of the guests in rapture.

At the end of these nights Morgan would slyly sneak me a warm plate of hand-rolled whole-wheat cavatelli with squab liver sautéed in vin santo and finished with roasted chestnuts. I think it was a kind of thank you for the opportunity to exercise his artistry to so many appreciative customers. We had a rocky relationship, but this was a gesture filled with love. Each bite of the dish made my head roll back into the universe; I had to steady myself when I landed back in my body. Something about the combination of the wild fat of the squab liver, the texture of the perfect pasta, the roundness and almost secretive flavor held in a chestnut, and the honeyed scent of the late-harvest wine unmoored me.

I guess it is the closest thing to an out-of-body experience food has ever given me.

Is there a way you want to feel on your deathbed?

"I have been pursued by people who have regarded me as the Death and Dying Lady," said Elisabeth Kübler-Ross. "They believe that having spent more than three decades in research into death and life after death qualifies me as an expert on the subject. I think they miss the point. The only incontrovertible fact of my work is the importance of life." There isn't a single human who has done more to wrench death and dying from the shadows and raise our death literacy than Swiss psychiatrist and author Elisabeth Kübler-Ross. She is to death and dying what Einstein was to science and physics. And by many accounts she died terribly. Several luminaries in the end-of-life sphere have told me that Elisabeth fought against death and that her death ultimately discredited her life's work.

According to one report: "Kübler-Ross sits in a cluttered corner of her home in the desert, smoking Dunhill cigarettes, watching TV and waiting to die . . . decades of work with the terminally ill has done little to ease her own transition into the great beyond . . . her German-accented voice is faint and tinged with bitterness . . . question(s) her own legacy and to reconsider her ideas about life, death and 'the other side.'"[1]

The only problem with this article and the luminaries who will remain unnamed is that they are apparently dead wrong. I have gotten to know Elisabeth's son Ken quite well, and I asked him, as Elisabeth's main caretaker, to relive those final years and days for me.

In 1994, at the age of sixty-eight, Elisabeth found herself in the middle of the AIDS crisis. It was a time when fears about the unknown disease circulated like wildfire. Elisabeth worked to create a hospice on her property in rural Virginia for abandoned babies infected with AIDS. This was not a popular idea with the locals, and her house was shot at, broken into, and vandalized. Elisabeth returned on an October afternoon from a speaking tour to find her house burnt to the ground and her favorite llama shot in the head. A lifetime's worth of possessions, gone.

Within a week her son Ken coaxed Elisabeth out to Scottsdale, but by Mother's Day she suffered a massive stroke and was paralyzed on the left side of her body. During her final nine years Elisabeth suffered from lack of mobility (which was very difficult for the spry and active seventy-year-old), painful neuropathy, related depression, and some very reasonable anger and bitterness at her loss of health and home.

"Fate had dealt her this crippling blow," Ken said, "and she was angry, but she never once renounced any of her theories. That is just ridiculous and goes in the category of things made up to sell papers. As my mother would say in her Swiss accent: bullshit.

"A few weeks before she passed she said to me: 'I'm not ready to die.' Which was surprising, given her readiness prior to this conversation, but she didn't elaborate." Ken said it took him a couple of years to understand what she meant. "One thing my mother always said was that when you learn your lessons, you're allowed to 'graduate.' She hadn't learned her final lesson, which was to allow herself to be loved and taken care of. This was hard for her to accept, to not always be the one in charge and to allow herself to be taken care of by others. And when my mother finally learned this last lesson, then she was allowed to 'graduate.'" Her family gave her palliative care, and she spent the last week of her life in and out of consciousness. "In accordance to her wishes that she wouldn't be in pain, we put her on morphine so she could pass peacefully," Ken said. "She died in the evening, in her home, with only my sister and me by her side."

Death is complex, and the death of an icon, especially a controversial one, gives rise to many emotions. But I believe the sentiment to flag here is death shaming. None of us can say until we get there how we will feel as we stare down our own death, and there are no "shoulds." Regardless of how Elisabeth felt when she died—which only she knows—why did anyone feel the urge to judge her for it? Death shaming is a real issue, not unlike the whispers of shame that go around surrounding birth. Was it a "good" birth? Does the new mother feel shamed if she used an epidural or had a C-section or was even unconscious during the birth of her child? We do the same thing surrounding death: Was it a "good" death? Did he cling to life when he "should" have let go? If it doesn't fit a script, blame is assigned.

"Most people aren't having these transformative deathbed moments," said B. J. Miller, former director of the Zen Hospice Center. "And if you hold that out as a goal, they're just going to feel like they're failing."[2]

Shame drips into every part of our lives, and death has some of the richest waters for it to dissolve. As bestselling author Dr. Brené Brown states, "Shame needs three things to grow: secrecy, silence, and judgment." These three components essentially sum up the death-and-dying world of the past fifty years, the world that Elisabeth worked so hard to bring into the light.

I lost a dear friend of mine ten years ago, and I remember how painful her memorial was. I couldn't bring myself to attend a postmemorial wake; drinking and telling stories about her were the opposite of what I needed. My decision hurt her daughter. She felt abandoned when I didn't attend. And to be clear, I understand her immense feelings of grief. However, what shame does is arrest; it's designed to freeze an action, and the judgment left me feeling paralyzed in my own grief. We shame our children when we want them to not only stop a particular behavior but also to feel badly about the fact that they committed the act in the first place. From a physiological perspective, shame throws us into fight, flight, or freeze. It is not a state where growth occurs. When we shame each other around death, we literally suspend our ability to heal or grow.

The fact is, just as with birth, we can't always control how things are going to go down. And we can't anticipate how we'll feel when they do. When there is great physical pain at the end of life, the overwhelming feeling might be a desire for release from that pain.

Ruth was terrified when she was dying. She was a Methodist who certainly had believed in heaven at some point, but now, as her heart gave out, she was frightened. The greatest kindness her daughter Margaret could offer her in her last days was to calm her. So Margaret took the vision of heaven she imagined Ruth would have and talked about it soothingly. She told Ruth about how, when she died, she'd step onto a field of grass, that her body would feel warmed by the sun. She calmed Ruth by telling her it was okay, that Margaret was okay, and that Ruth's late husband was on the grass waiting for her. Never mind that Margaret didn't herself believe a word of it—that hardly mattered. She wanted to remove the feeling of fear from her mom's last moments as best she could.

When Oliver Sacks learned he had a terminal illness, he wrote that he felt not only fear but also "a sudden clear focus and perspective. There is no time for anything inessential. I must focus on myself, my work and my friends. I shall no longer look at 'NewsHour' every night. I shall no longer pay any attention to politics or arguments about global warming." It wasn't that he no longer cared, he explained, but rather that they were the problems of the future, and his focus was sharpened on the now. But again, I would argue that this, too, cannot be anticipated. Sacks wrote, "It is the fate—the genetic and neural fate—of every human being to be a unique individual, to find his own path, to live his own life, to die his own death."[3]

I can't get away from the parallels between birth and death and have long wondered what the research on one can share about the other. Anne Drapkin Lyerly tackled the issue of what constitutes a good birth through an extensive research project that became the foundation for her book *A Good Birth*. She found that the common ground of the good birth was not to be found in midwifery versus birthing center versus hospital but rather in what lay beneath it all: control, agency, personal security, connectedness, respect, and knowledge. We can't always offer these to the dying, nor can we ourselves always have access. But we can try. And we can offer comfort, empathy, and a stance of nonjudgment. Elisabeth showed us the path so many years ago. Now we just need to continue to follow her.

What would you want people to say about you at your funeral?

The "think about what you want written on your tombstone" advice is nothing new. And yet how often do you have that conversation with those you love? I had a pretty remarkable chance to experience my own living funeral and to take this thinking to the next level. In lieu of a fortieth birthday party, my friends threw me a living funeral. I ended up learning more about what it means to receive love than finding a few pithy words to cast in stone.

Our heart has two primary functions. Half the heart is designed for receiving, welcoming, taking in the nutrient-rich material, moving it through our lungs so that it is once again oxygenated. The other half is built with a completely different function: to pump the blood back out, distributing it with exceptional accuracy and force. Heart attacks occur when the timing goes haywire, when our ability to give and receive is out of balance. Heart disease is still the number-one killer in the United States.[1]

Our culture places a premium on expressing love, hugging, showing gratitude, giving praise—not that everyone practices it, but it is present as a kind of cultural imperative. What isn't discussed, instructed about, or blogged about as much is *receiving* love. Accepting love and appreciation is hard work. I was three months from my fortieth birthday when the love of my life and I decided that we needed to take a break, perhaps forever. As the break began to become real, a growing specter appeared on my emotional horizon: my upcoming birthday. As soon as I acknowledged the dark emotional figure, a veil of sadness dropped from the rainy October gloom on Vashon Island, where we had been living together for three years. Was I really going to spend my fortieth alone? Would I have to face this rite of passage, this great reflective point, as a single man, surrounded by memories of broken relationships? This woman whom I considered my life partner, gone?

I am not a big fan of processing discomfort alone, so I immediately emailed my favorite people, asking them to save my birthday weekend on their calendars. It would be a lost weekend somewhere along the northern Californian coast, I promised. I didn't give more details. Could any of them make it? Luckily forty "yes" RSVPs filled my inbox within a day, and I didn't have to sit in the terror of my impending solitude. One week later an email ripped through the birthday list from one of my oldest, most irreverent friends, Matt Wiggins.

"Wigs" was calling for a living funeral. He thought that we should honor my great turn by having me play dead for multiple hours while my dear ones aired their grievances and offered loving eulogies. Many people have said that they wish they could be at their own funeral. It was starting to look like I was going to join Tom Sawyer and Augustus Waters and be present at a version of mine.

The day I was to die dawned after an evening of feasting and musical performances that would make a prince green with envy. Everyone took the preparations seriously—and so did I. I spent the day in relative solitude, breaking for a long massage, eating little, spending hours in meditation, in and out of a sauna and cold baths, anointing myself with appropriate oils and dressing in flowing white. Because how often do we get to prepare for our own funeral, right?

Dusk inched up the hill and, with my eyes closed, I was led to step into what I soon understood was a coffin, thankfully open, and the shuffle of feet and heft of gravity made it clear that a crew of pallbearers was soldiered on either side. I laughed uneasily, realizing that my friends had taken this endeavor to a whole new level and commissioned a cedar coffin just for the occasion.

The warm, sour smell of whiskey washed over me. I smiled thinking about the bottle that I am sure went around to all the pallbearers. The coffin landed with a whisper, and only a single candle flickered in the space. I didn't open my eyes, but I knew by the pale darkness along my inner eyelids that my friends were hidden in obscura.

Kathy Maxwell, Wigs's mom, broke the shuffling silence and reminded us that we were on Miwok land and told the assembly that she had recently hosted the funeral for a tribal elder in this very room. She let us know that she had chosen their elegant ritual as a model for our gathering. As she mentioned my name, a friend began to wail, not in jest, but in the type of painful sobs that are rare at real funerals.

For the next three hours I was as still as a leaf. The only indulgence I couldn't avoid were the tears that welled into pools, so that my eyelids were partly submerged much of the time. People spoke first of how they knew me. The pain of loss shot through with outrageous humor and candor. Grievances and eulogies came next, and the grievances that bubbled up were real, lanced with hurt—and for each of them I was grateful. I found that I could easily process the emotional hardships, the miscommunications, the regrettable moments. I got to see where my heart connection was in jeopardy with my close friends, how they saw me, and who I needed to apologize to, who I needed to more generously show myself to, knowing that after I jumped out of the coffin I could polish each heart connection until it gleamed.

What hit me like a truck was the love. The unbearable, unalloyed, full-throttle love that poured from the lips of these people I admire most. It was simply too much: it felt burning hot at moments, my skin aflame, and I had nowhere to hide. These people loved me. They saw me for my genuine heart, saw my misgivings and gaping holes, and loved the beejezus out of me anyway. I couldn't deflect, I couldn't change the channel, I couldn't even blush or thank them—I just had to receive.

And then it dawned on me.

If I don't know how to properly receive love, then what could I possibly know about being alive? I was only using one side of my heart—giving love, taking care of people (and avoiding those who I didn't want to love anymore). I had built up this massive muscle—unbalanced and in danger. I didn't arrive at a pithy epitaph that day, but what this bizarre gift did provide was the clear directive that receiving love is where I needed to focus my attention. Once again, reflecting on death did not give rise to the macabre but instead gave me some clear direction about how to live, now, in the present.

This is what I took away from attending my own funeral, but the broader message, I believe, is that holding a living funeral is an incredible opportunity to grow—though the form of that growth will look different for each person.

I was lucky that I got to step out of that coffin at the end of the day. Many others who choose to attend their own funeral do so because they know they are dying soon and, dammit, want to attend the party in their honor. That's what happened with Mary Elizabeth Williams's friend Jessica, who was dying of cancer. She initially planned to have a small birthday party, but guests arrived to an empty home when she had to be rushed to the hospital. That's when she changed the focus. "I want to get everybody together," Jessica said. "I want to hear all the nice things." And hear them she did—from her husband, who explained he knew the first evening they met that she would be the love of his life, to the singing of "Space Oddity" around a piano.

"What if, whenever possible, we leaned in toward mortality a little more?" her friend Mary Elizabeth wondered. "What if we stopped pretending, until the last breath was drawn, that it was all going to get better? What if we gave the experience some space, not just for ourselves to grieve, but for the person who's dying to grieve too? . . . . It takes unbelievable gumption and heart to say, this is it, so hold me and tell me you love me. It takes strength to invite death in and to know when to stop raging against the dying light. To not put on a happy face and not to make any more plans together and just sit with the truth that one of you is leaving."[2]

John Shields also decided to do just that when he was in the last days of his life. Terminally ill, he was taking advantage of Canada's medically assisted suicide laws and had a date he was scheduled to die. He thought he might like to have an Irish wake the night before. There would be music and drinking and roasting and toasting.

"One after another," wrote Catherine Porter, in a piece about John for the *New York Times*, "proclamations of love, admiration, and gratitude poured forth. They thanked their host for opening his door when they were brokenhearted. They thanked him for his friendship. They thanked him for his courage."[3]

He got to hear all of that. He got to thank them in return. And then he got to say good-bye, smiling at everyone as he said, "I will see you later."

How do you end a conversation about death?

Together we have walked through many dark canyons in this book, places we don't often go, alone or even with friends. And I know I have said it before, but it is a simple truth that bears repeating: there are no easy answers as we head into this territory. There is a compass, though, and I think that compass is gratitude.

How we end conversations about death is critical, regardless of whether we are at a beautiful table or driving on the interstate. It is important that people feel emotionally safe when discussing end of life, and gratitude connects human hearts. I'm reminded of the sage words of Stephen Jenkinson, "Gratitude needs practice." It is the foremost reason why I begin each death dinner with an acknowledgment of our ancestors and why I end each dinner with admiration for the living, called an "appreciation in the round." Appreciation in the round is a ritual that has circled the globe hundreds of times, but it began with Kathy Maxwell and a daily practice she used to bring some civility to her home dinner table.

A couple of days before her son Charlie's first communion, Kathy poked her head into a knick-knack store in Darien, Connecticut, looking for something to commemorate the important ritual. "I went in and saw this handmade chalice that said around the edges, 'You are a child of God forever.'" It seemed perfect, and as she brought it home she had an idea. As any single parent knows, dinnertime can begin to make you feel like a prison warden, and Kathy had three extraordinarily precocious kids. So she thought she'd fill the chalice with grape juice at dinner the night of the communion and tell her kids that they were going to play a new game called "The Blessing Cup." Before they were allowed to dig in to the meal, everyone had to pass the cup around and say something nice about everyone at the table, then take a sip of the grape juice. In a rather remarkable way Kathy brought communion home to her family.

In the beginning she had to coach her kids a little, but in time they took full ownership of the nightly ritual. As each child made a home for themselves, Kathy gifted them with a Blessing Cup of their own. Kathy makes each cup out of clay—her granddaughter has become her cup-making apprentice—and she hand-paints "come to the table" around the edge of each chalice.

Regardless of your spiritual identity, the effect of giving daily affirmations to your family—or anyone, for that matter—can be transformative. The version we practice at death dinners is not seen as a communion, and we don't ask people to pass a chalice, but we do end every dinner with this idea. When we discuss intense topics, especially topics we tend to repress, we need to be thoughtful about the container we create around the conversation and how we invite people to re-enter the normal not-talking-about-death world. We want to give a sense of closure—people need to know when it's okay to head home—and to complete the experience with a small rush of oxytocin that our body naturally creates when we feel loved or appreciated.

To initiate the appreciation, someone shares something they appreciate about the person directly on their right or left. You never pre-assign who is going to go first; you just let it happen. The person who begins only picks one person to appreciate, and when you are being appreciated, your only job is to receive what is being said. It might be a new acquaintance sitting next to you, and the appreciation of you might be about your fabulous shoes. The trick is to take it in, not deflect, not appreciate them back— just say thank you. And then turn to the person next to you and reach down inside yourself and say something that you truly admire about them. Maybe it's your life partner and you haven't had a chance to fully appreciate them for years. Say something that feels risky and emotional—I promise you: if it's a genuine appreciation, it will be meaningful. Once the circle completes, people who need to leave will feel comfortable saying their good-byes.

I WAITED ALMOST FIVE YEARS before I hosted a death dinner with my mom and brother. I have been around the globe hosting dinners, and yet I still hadn't sent the two most important invites. So, in short, I understand that this is difficult work, and I don't profess to be some kind of exemplary end-of-life citizen. Although I have spent twenty years working around the clock to "reinvigorate the dinner table," I find great joy in eating in bed with my two daughters and watching *Parks and Recreation*.

It felt profoundly awkward as we all sat down to the table. I know how to host strangers or friends, but there was something almost too intimate about having flesh and blood at the table. This was heightened by the fact that there were only four of us. My twelve-year-old nephew Finn joined us. I had suggested to my brother beforehand that we set him up with a pizza and a movie, but he wanted to include Finn. But my brother had had a crazy day at work and had forgotten to give him any prep. So we began the dinner by explaining to Finn what the conversation was going to be covering that night. When Finn understood that we were talking about death, he stood up and left—immediately.

We were breaking at least a couple of my golden rules: Never surprise someone with a death dinner or even a conversation about death. Consent is key. And only include children if they have expressed a strong desire to be present. So, in short, things were going terribly.

Finn came back halfway through the dinner to quickly eat his food and to let us know he thought the idea was awful. "Why would you ruin a perfectly good meal where people are enjoying themselves by talking about 'it'?" he asked. Finn was so uncomfortable with death that he wouldn't say the word, or so my brother explained to us as Finn quickly left the table again.

Despite these seeming calamities, it was, without question, the most meaningful, memorable, and simply enjoyable meal I have ever had with my mom and brother.

What it made it so? Finn's coming and going couldn't shake the depth of conversation happening at the table. There was no bickering. Everyone actually listened to each other. I saw the best characteristics in both of my kin. Their genius shined through. My mom, once again, apologized for not being a better mother, admitted that she had done very little to share her life story with us, and then reflected thoughtfully on how we couldn't possibly understand her if we didn't know the events and life experience that shaped her and how hard it must have been to respect her parental choices without knowing who she truly was. My brother Brian's exceptional ability with words and emotion was on fine display, and I was struck by his utter candor and reflections. I wish I had recorded the evening, as his thoughts were some of the most insightful I've heard at any death conversation yet.

For me it was a profound moment of not feeling like a refugee. I have always felt not quite like an orphan but, in a way, separate from my nuclear family. But last night—and it was last night as I write this—I could see very clearly how the qualities I like most about myself had their origin in these two lovely human beings. My mother's exceptional defiance of the establishment, her unwillingness to take anything for granted, her incredible strength of character and independence. Where I would otherwise notice her stubbornness and negativity, last night I saw her better angels, clearly and gloriously. And I could tell that my mom and Brian felt equally seen, like the three of us had witnessed each other, all just via the trick of four simple questions I asked at the table, all pulled from this book, and based upon which seemed most right at the given moment. I had written a detailed script before dinner, carefully considering which questions to ask, but

I didn't follow it. It seemed better to pull the questions from memory, responding to the direction of our conversation.

We did, however, begin with acknowledging those who we have lost, and we ended with an appreciation in the round.

Over two thousand years ago the philosopher Epicurus, who also had a deep passion for the table, taught that death denial was the principal root of all human neurosis and acknowledged our vulnerable relationship to our own mortality, famously writing, "Against other things it is possible to obtain security, but when it comes to death we human beings all live in an unwalled city." In this unwalled city we have the opportunity to learn so much about ourselves and each other. It is a conversation that expands our understanding of compassion and has the capacity to connect us more poignantly than any topic I have encountered. As Ram Dass reminds us, "We are all just walking each other home."

I love to think about the thousands of people who have held these conversations, and one of my favorite images is that of a family or even a single individual washing dishes and blowing out the candles at the end of an evening. Reflecting on what their friends and loved ones said as they felt their way into new territory together. It drives home the truth that there is no one way to end a conversation about death, and there is no one way to talk about death. Death walks with us through our entire life. The best thing I can suggest is that we all get better acquainted with our constant companion.

ACKNOWLEDGMENTS

First and foremost, to my intrepid cowriter Jenna Land Free: without her brilliance, clarity, and perseverance, this book would still just be a sketch in a Google doc in the cloud somewhere. Our joyous and wise editor, Renée Sedliar, as well as Miriam Riad, and our warrior agent Gail Ross, who believed in this book way before she should have. Thank you to Richard Harris for getting this process started and for introducing me to Gail. Thank you to the rest of my publishing team at Hachette: Michael Pietsch, Susan Weinberg, John Radziewicz, Lissa Warren, Kevin Hanover, Alex Camlin, Josephine Moore, and Christine Marra. My cofounder, best friend, and constant spiritual companion, Angel Grant, who lit so many of these dark canyons with astounding insight and compassion. The remarkable guidance of my friends and early readers—Debra Music, Lesley Hazleton, Tiffany Wendel, Maya Lockwood, Eleanor Cleverly, Dream Hampton—who polished this book over countless hours. I'm also so, so appreciative for the dozens of people who agreed to openly and vulnerably share their stories for this book. I'm humbled by their trust.

Thanks to my daughters, August and Violet, who taught me how to say things straight from the heart and put up with me as I knuckled through these pages. The mothers of my daughters for bringing such extraordinary humans into the world. And to every last Death Over Dinner advocate and adviser and to every single person who has the courage to pick up a book called *Let's Talk About Death* or attend a death dinner.

To my early partners in Death Over Dinner, Michael Ellsworth and Corey Gutch, and the design firm Civilization, and Scott Macklin for championing this at the University of Washington against great odds. A tremendous thank you to our partners in Australia, Rebecca Bartel and Deakin University; and our partner in Brazil, Tom Almeida; and Krittika Sharma and Sanam Singh in India. And best for last, a final thank you to Sunny Singh and my partners at RoundGlass for sharing this work with millions across the globe.

RECOMMENDATIONS FOR
FURTHER READING

Being Mortal: Medicine and What Matters in the End. Atul Gawande.

Being with Dying: Cultivating Compassion and Fearlessness in the Presence of Death. Joan Halifax and Ira Byock.

The Cost of Hope: A Memoir. Amanda Bennett.

The Death Class: A True Story About Life. Erika Hayasaki.

The December Project: An Extraordinary Rabbi and a Skeptical Seeker Confront Life's Greatest Mystery. Sara Davidson.

The Deepest Well: Healing the Long-Term Effects of Childhood Adversity. Dr. Nadine Burke Harris.

Die Wise. Stephen Jenkinson.

Dying Well: Peace and Possibilities at the End of Life. Ira Byock.

The End of Your Life Book Club. Mary Anne Schwalbe.

Extreme Measures: Finding a Better Path to the End of Life. Dr. Jessica Nutik Zitter, MD.

Final Gifts: Understanding the Special Awareness, Needs, and Communications of the Dying. Maggie Callanan and Patricia Kelley.

The Five Invitations: What the Living Can Learn from the Dying. Frank Ostaseski.

The Four Things That Matter Most: A Book About Living. Ira Byock.

From Here to Eternity: Traveling the World to Find the Good Death. Caitlin Doughty.

God's Hotel: A Doctor, a Hospital, and a Pilgrimage to the Heart of Medicine. Victoria Sweet.

Knocking on Heaven's Door. Katy Butler.

The Last Lecture. Randy Pausch.

Mortality. Christopher Hitchens.

On Death and Dying: What the Dying Have to Teach Doctors, Nurses, Clergy and Their Own Families. Elisabeth Kübler Ross.

Smoke Gets in Your Eyes: And Other Lessons from the Crematory. Caitlin Doughty.

Standing at the Edge: Finding Freedom Where Fear and Courage Meet. Joan Halifax and Rebecca Solnit.

Stiff: The Curious Lives of Human Cadavers. Mary Roach.

Still Here: Embracing Aging, Changing, and Dying. Ram Dass.

The Tibetan Book of the Dead: The Great Book of Natural Liberation Through Understanding in the Between. Padma Sambhava (compiler), Robert Thurman (translator), the Dalai Lama (foreword), Karma Lingpa (collaborator).

When Breath Becomes Air. Paul Kalanithi.

When the Body Says No: Understanding the Stress-Disease Connection. Gabor Maté.

Who Dies? An Investigation of Conscious Living and Conscious Dying. Stephen Levine.

The Wild Edge of Sorrow: Rituals of Renewal and the Sacred Work of Grief. Francis Weller.

The Year of Magical Thinking. Joan Didion.

A Year to Live: How to Live This Year as If It Were Your Last. Stephen Levine.

OUR FAMILY OF RESOURCES

Our Death Over Dinner team has combined forces with global wellness organization RoundGlass to expand and deepen our interactive platforms and end-of-life resources.

Death Over Dinner. www.deathoverdinner.org.
The website that sparked this book and includes everything you need to start and host a conversation over dinner about end of life.

Death Over Dinner—Doctors and Nurses. www.deathoverdinner.org/medical.
Our collaboration with dozens of medical leaders in the United States, designed for medical professionals.

Death Over Dinner—Jewish Edition. www.deathoverdinner-jewishedition.org.
Our collaboration with REBOOT, IKAR, Rabbi Sharon Brous, and over thirty rabbis.

Death Over Dinner—Australian Edition. www.deathoverdinner.org.au.
Our collaboration with dozens of medical leaders in Australia.

Death Over Dinner—Brazil. www.deathoverdinner.org.br.
Our collaboration with dozens of medical and spiritual leaders in Brazil.

Death Over Dinner—India. www.deathoverdinner.org.in.
Our collaboration with dozens of medical and spiritual leaders in India.

Living Wake. www.livewake.com.
A tool kit to host a living wake or living funeral for the people we love while they are still alive.

The Endless Table. www.endlesstable.org.
A collection of recipes from and memories of departed loved ones.

Death Questions. www.deathquestions.org.
We asked hundreds of end-of-life experts every question about death and dying we could think of—the responses are remarkable.

Death Reading Room. www.deathreadingroom.com.
An up-to-date resource of articles, podcasts, talks, and other short-form content focused on end of life.

The Will Bank. www.thewillbank.org.
A place to create and store your living will, advance-care directives, healthcare proxies, and last will and testament.

WeDie. www.wedie.org.
A singular site meant for individuals to step into an empowered relationship with their eventual deaths—and to make informed decisions and conscious purchases.

Additional Resources

Advance Directive for Dementia.
www.dementia-directive.org.
A simple way to document the medical care you desire, if you are or a loved one is suffering from early-onset Alzheimer's or dementia.

Aspire. www.aspirehealthcare.com.
A network of specialized physician practices that provide comprehensive medical care in the home for patients facing a serious illness.

Before I Die. www.beforeidie.city.
A global participatory public art project that reimagines our relationship with death and with one another.

Calico. www.calicolabs.com.
Calico is a research and development company whose mission is to harness advanced technologies to increase our understanding of the biology that controls life span.

Coeio. www.coeio.com.
The Infinity Burial Suit is a green funeral product that benefits the earth by cleansing toxins found in the body and soil and helping plants grow better.

Coffin Clubs. www.loadingdocs.net/thecoffinclub.
A group of rebellious, creative Kiwi seniors give death the finger, one crazy coffin at a time.

The Conversation Project. www.theconversationproject.org.
An extensive set of resources dedicated to helping people talk about their wishes for end-of-life care.

The Dinner Party. www.thedinnerparty.org.
A community of mostly twenty- and thirtysomethings who've each experienced significant loss and get together over dinner parties to talk about it and the ways in which it continues to affect their lives.

Elisabeth Kübler-Ross Foundation. www.ekrfoundation.org.
The foundation that carries on the work of the great end of life pioneer.

End of Life University. www.eoluniversity.com.
An interview series that consists of in-depth educational interviews with experts from all aspects of end of life.

Everplans. www.everplans.com.
A secure, digital archive of wills, trusts, and insurance policies; important accounts and passwords; advance directives and DNRs; final wishes and funeral preferences.

Future File. www.futurefile.com.
A comprehensive and easy-to-use system for legacy planning.

GYST. www.gyst.com.
An online service to help get your end-of-life documents in order, one step at a time, starting with your will, living will/advance directive, and life insurance.

The Longevity Prize. www.paloaltoprize.com.
The Palo Alto Longevity Prize is a $1 million life science competition dedicated to ending aging.

Meet Grace. www.meetgrace.com.
An excellent online hospice and assisted-living directory.

Modern Loss. www.modernloss.com.
A website offering candid content, resources, and community on loss and grief.

National Suicide Prevention Lifeline (US).
www.suicidepreventionlifeline.org.
The Lifeline provides 24/7, free, and confidential support for people in distress, prevention and crisis resources for you or your loved ones, and best practices for professionals.

The Order of the Good Death. www.orderofthegooddeath.com.
A group of funeral industry professionals, academics, and artists exploring ways to prepare a death-phobic culture for their inevitable mortality.

Recompose. www.recompose.life.
Recompose is developing a process that gently converts human remains into soil so that we can nourish new life after we die. Our goal is to offer recompositon as an alternative choice to cremation and conventional burial.

Tomorrow. www.tomorrow.me.
A user-friendly mobile app where you can create a will, determine guardianship, and purchase life insurance.

Veterans Struggling with PTSD (US). www.ptsd.va.gov.
A tremendous resource dedicated to research and education on trauma and PTSD.

Vital Talk. www.vitaltalk.org.
A dynamic organization led by physicians that teaches end-of-life communication skills to medical practitioners.

We Croak. www.wecroak.com.
A mobile app based on a Bhutanese folk saying that to be a happy person, one must contemplate death five times daily.

Zen Hospice Mindful Caregiver Education. www.zenhospice.org.
A program that offers social, medical, and spiritual practices to enable professional and family caregivers to experience compassion and resiliency at the bedside while reducing burnout and enhancing care.

NOTES

Chapter 1. Offering Permission

1. Amy S. Kelley, Kathleen McGarry, Sean Fahle, Samuel M. Marshall, Qingling Du, and Jonathan S. Skinner, "Out-of-Pocket Spending in the Last Five Years of Life," *Journal of General Internal Medicine* 28, no. 2 (February 2013): 304–309.

2. "Where Do Americans Die?" Stanford School of Medicine, Palliative Care, https://palliative.stanford.edu/home-hospice-home-care -of-the-dying-patient/where-do-americans-die.

3. "Of 122 medical schools researchers surveyed more recently, only eight had mandatory coursework in end-of-life care." Susan Svrluga, "Doctors Need to Learn About Dying, Too," *Washington Post*, January 15, 2016, www.washingtonpost.com/news/grade-point/wp /2016/01/15/doctors-need-to-learn-about-dying-too/?noredirect =on&utm_term=.8324597d6ac9. "When asked how well their basic nursing education prepared them for providing EOL care, 71% rated pain management education as inadequate, 62% rated overall content of EOL care as inadequate. Because of these deficiencies, EOL dilemmas and barriers to providing high quality EOL care are common in nursing practice." Kathy Hebert, Harold Moore, and Joan Rooney, "The Nurse Advocate in End-of-Life Care," *Ochsner Journal* 11, no. 4 (Winter 2011): 325–329.

4. "Elder Abuse Statistics," Nursing Home Abuse Center, www .nursinghomeabusecenter.com/elder-abuse/statistics.

5. Gina Roberts-Grey, "Keeping Secrets Can Be Hazardous to Your Health," *Forbes*, October 24, 2013, www.forbes.com/sites/nextavenue /2013/10/24/keeping-secrets-can-be-hazardous-to-your-health.

6. "Cortisol," You and Your Hormones, www.yourhormones.info /hormones/cortisol.

7. Christopher R. Longwood and Dara N. Greenwood. "Joking in the Face of Death: A Terror Management Approach to Humor Production," *Humor: International Journal of Humor Research* 26, no. 4 (2013): 493–510.

8. "'Tuesdays with Morrie' Author Mitch Albom on Morrie's Lasting Lessons," *CBS This Morning*, May 12, 2017, www.cbsnews.com/news /tuesdays-with-morrie-author-mitch-albom-lasting-impact.

Chapter 2: Extending the Invitation

1. From a presentation at "The Death Salon," Seattle, Washington, September 10, 2017.

The Prompts

If you had only thirty days left to live, how would you spend them? Your last day? Your last hour?

1. Pang-Hsiang Liu, Mary Beth Landrum, Jane C. Weeks, Haiden A. Huskamp, Katherine L. Kahn, Yulei He, Jennifer W. Mack et al., "Physicians' Propensity to Discuss Prognosis Is Associated with Patients' Awareness of Prognosis for Metastatic Cancers," *Journal of Palliative Medicine* 17, no. 6 (June 2014): 673–682.

Is there an excess of medical intervention at the end of life?

1. Jay Baruch, "I'm an Ambassador to Nightmares. My Medical Training Didn't Prepare Me for That," *STAT*, September 7, 2017, www .statnews.com/2017/09/07/emergency-physician-death-families.

2. Neil Orford, "Give Death Its Due in a System Focused on Life," *Sydney Morning Herald*, July 7, 2015, www.smh.com.au/comment/hospitals-must-shift-focus-of-endoflife-care-from-disease-to-people-20150706-gi6joz.html.

3. Ashleigh Witt, "The Day I Meet You in the Emergency Department Will Probably Be One of the Worst of Your Life," *Sydney Morning Herald*, November 6, 2015, www.smh.com.au/national/the-day-i-meet-you-in-the-emergency-department-will-probably-be-one-of-the-worst-of-your-life-20151105-gkrbm7.html.

4. The opinions expressed herein are Dr. Jackson's and do not represent the views of the University of Washington or UW Medicine.

5. Christine Cowgill, "Urgent Need for Better End-of-Life Training," *Today's Geriatric Medicine*, June 26, 2013; www.todaysgeriatricmedicine.com/news/ex_062613.shtml.

6. Chris Hayhurst, "Why Providers Are Slow to Adopt New Medicare Codes," *AthenaInsight,* November 9, 2017, www.athenahealth.com/insight/why-providers-are-slow-adopt-new-medicare-codes.

7. Catherine Lee Hough, Leonard D. Hudson, Antonio Salud, Timothy Lahey, and J. Randall Curtis, "Death Rounds: End-of-Life Discussions Among Medical Residents in the Intensive Care Unit," *Journal of Critical Care* 20, no. 1 (March 2005): 20–25.

8. Colleen F. Manning, Michelle Acker, Laura Houseman, Emilee Pressman, and Irene Goodman, "Schwartz Center Rounds Evaluation Report: Executive Summary," Goodman Research Group, February 2008, www.theschwartzcenter.org/media/PTXAAE65CHR5UU4.pdf.

9. Ira Byock, "At the End of Life, What Would Doctors Do?" *New York Times*, June 30, 2016, https://well.blogs.nytimes.com/2016/06/30/at-the-end-of-life-what-would-doctors-do.

What is the most significant end-of-life experience of which you've been a part?

1. Laurie Anderson, "Laurie Anderson's Farewell to Lou Reed," *Rolling Stone*, November 6, 2013, www.rollingstone.com/music/news/laurie-andersons-farewell-to-lou-reed-a-rolling-stone-exclusive-20131106.

Why don't we talk about death?

1. See Gabor Maté, *When the Body Says No: Exploring the Stress-Disease Connection* (New York: Wiley, 2011). Also see Sandra P. Thomas, Maureen Groer, Mitzi Davis, Patricia Droppleman, Johnie Mozingo, and Margaret Pierce, "Anger and Cancer: An Analysis of the Linkages," *Cancer Nursing* 23, no. 5 (October 2000): 344–349; FJ Penedo, et al. "Anger Suppression Mediates the Relationship Between Optimism and Natural Killer Cell Cytotoxicity in Men Treated for Localized Prostate Cancer," *Journal of Psychosomatic Research* 60, no. 4 (April 2006): 423–427; Petty Reynolds, Susan Hurley, Myriam Torres, James Jackson, Peggy Boyd, and Vivien W. Chen, "Use of Coping Strategies and Breast Cancer Survival: Results from the Black/White Cancer Survival Study," *American Journal of Epidemiology* 152, no. 10 (November 2000): 940–949.

2. Author Michael Lewis famously grappled with the subject in both *Money Ball* and *The Undoing Project*, where he showed us the misguided thinking in the sports world when it came to spotting talent and selecting the right draft picks. It turns out computers and algorithms are better at producing a World Series win than relying on our own thinking, our own gut instincts and "rational minds."

3. Pang-Hsiang Liu, Mary Beth Landrum, Jane C. Weeks, Haiden A. Huskamp, Katherine L. Kahn, Yulei He, Jennifer W. Mack et al., "Physicians' Propensity to Discuss Prognosis Is Associated with Patients' Awareness of Prognosis for Metastatic Cancers," *Journal of Palliative Medicine* 17, no. 6 (June 2014): 673–682.

4. Daniel Kahnemann, *Thinking, Fast and Slow* (New York: Farrar, Straus, and Giroux, 2013).

5. Edward L. Bennett, Marian C. Diamond, David Krech, and Mark R. Rosenzweig, "Chemical and Anatomical Plasticity of Brain," *Science* 146, no. 3644 (October 30, 1964): 610–619.

Do you believe in an afterlife?

1. Francesca E. Duncan, Emily L. Que, Nan Zhang, Eve C. Feinberg, Thomas V. O'Halloran, and Teresa K. Woodruff, "The Zinc Spark

Is an Inorganic Signature of Human Egg Activation," *Scientific Reports* 6, no. 1 (July 2016): 24737.

Would you ever consider doctor-assisted suicide?

1. Ira Byock, "We Should Think Twice About 'Death with Dignity,'" *Los Angeles Times*, January 30, 2015, www.latimes.com/opinion/op-ed/la-oe-0201-byock-physician-assisted-suicide-20150201-story.html.

2. For more information see Robert Sapolsky, *Why Zebras Don't Get Ulcers*, 3rd ed. (New York: Holt Paperbacks, 2004). See also William R. Stixrud and Ned Johnson, *The Self-Driven Child: The Science and Sense of Giving Your Kids More Control Over Their Lives* (New York: Viking, 2018).

3. Mary J. Ruwart, "Assisted Suicide Doesn't Take Lives . . . It Saves Them," *FinalExit Network Newsletter* 16, no. 3 (Summer 2017).

What song would you want played at your funeral? Who would sing it?

1. Questlove, "On the Passing of Richard Nichols, the First Voice in My Book," Vulture.com, July 20, 2014, www.vulture.com/2014/07/questlove-richard-nichols-tribute-obit.html.

2. "Richard" is on the album *Promise* and was released by Thesis & Instinct Records in 2016.

What do you want done with your body?

1. From Tanya Marsh's presentation at "The Death Salon," Seattle, Washington, September 10, 2017.

2. Ibid.

3. Dan McComb, "The Coffinmaker," *Vimeo*, https://vimeo.com/65019294.

Are there certain deaths we should never speak of?

1. Stephen Levine, *A Year to Live: How to Live This Year as If It Were Your Last* (New York: Harmony, 1997).

If you could extend your life, how many years would you add?
Twenty, fifty, one hundred, forever?

1. "Erectile Dysfunction Drugs Market Worth $3.2 Billion by 2022," Grand View Research, July 2016, www.grandviewresearch.com /press-release/global-erectile-dysfunction-drugs-market.

What do you want your legacy to be?

1. Paul Kalanithi, *When Breath Becomes Air* (New York: Random House, 2016).

How long should we grieve?

1. Cora Neumann, "No One Tells You This About Loss, So I Will," *Huffington Post*, June 1, 2016, www.huffingtonpost.com/cora-neumann /no-one-tells-you-this-about-loss-so-i-will_b_10154122.html.

2. Caitlin Doughty, *Smoke Gets in Your Eyes: And Other Lessons from the Crematory* (New York: W. W. Norton, 2015).

Is there a way you want to feel on your deathbed?

1. Don Lattin, "Expert on Death Faces Her Own Death / Kubler-Ross Now Questions Her Life's Work," *San Francisco Gate*, May 31, 1997, www.sfgate.com/news/article/Expert-On-Death-Faces-Her -Own-Death-Kubler-Ross-2837216.php.

2. Jon Mooallem, "One Man's Quest to Change the Way We Die," *New York Times* magazine, January 3, 2017, www.nytimes.com/2017 /01/03/magazine/one-mans-quest-to-change-the-way-we-die.html.

3. Oliver Sacks, "My Own Life," *New York Times*, February 19, 2015, www.nytimes.com/2015/02/19/opinion/oliver-sacks-on-learning -he-has-terminal-cancer.html.

What would you want people to say about you at your funeral?

1. "Underlying Cause of Death, 1999–2013," CDC, https:// wonder.cdc.gov/ucd-icd10.html. Data are from the Multiple Cause of Death Files, 1999–2013, as compiled from data provided by the

fifty-seven vital statistics jurisdictions through the Vital Statistics Co-operative Program.

2. Mary Elizabeth Williams, "Have Your Funeral Before You Die," *Salon*, January 28, 2018, www.salon.com/2018/01/28/have-your -funeral-before-you-die.

3. Catherine Porter, "At His Own Wake, Celebrating Life and the Gift of Death," *New York Times*, May 25, 2017, www.nytimes.com/2017 /05/25/world/canada/euthanasia-bill-john-shields-death.html.

INDEX

Adams, Jody, 53
Adler, Jonathan, 57
afterlife belief, 108–116
    Angel's experience, 109–111
    Carine McCandless's experience,
      111–112
    Cynthia's experience, 110–111
    letting go, 110
    Maya Lockwood's experience,
      114–116
    messages from dead loved ones, 108,
      110, 113
    Michael Hebb's experience, 108
    Monica's experience, 112–113
    near-death experiences, 114–116
Agarwal, Alpa, 150–152
Albom, Mitch, 15
Algordanza, 155
Alzheimer's, 6–7, 147
Anderson, Laurie, 80
Andrea, 60–61
Andrés, José, 50–51
anger, 201
appreciation in the round, 216–218
Arnold, Jenna, 136–137
attunement, 69
Ayahuasca or Aya, 97

Back, Anthony "Tony," 67, 69–70,
    121–123
Baruch, Jay, 63

base-rate bias (or base-rate neglect), 99
Bates, Briar, 58–60
Beaverton, Oregon, 117
Becker, Ernest, 177, 178
Being Mortal (Gawande), 7, 37
Benedict XVI (Pope Emeritus), 135
Berry, Wendell, 33
bioresilience, 171–172
Bios Urns, 155
Blessing Cup, 216–217
Bloomsbury Group, 28
body, disposition of, 147–158
    Alpa Agarwal's experience, 150–152
    Cassandra Yonder's experience,
      156–158
    coffins, 153–154
    community deathcare, 157
    cremation, 152–153, 155
    death rituals in India, 149–151
    green burials, 153
    home funerals, 156–157
    importance of ritual, 154
    Infinity Burial Suit, 154–155
    non-medicalized guidance through
      death process, 158
    Scott Kreiling's experience, 147–149
Boise, Idaho, 84
A Botany of Desire (Pollan), 176
Bowie, David, 124
Brain Games (TV show), 174
Brand, Stewart, 184

Brous, David, 193–194

Brous, Sharon, 193–194

Brown, Brené, 208

Brownlow, Morgan, 204–205

Bud, 184–185

Byock, Ira, 62, 71, 119

California, right-to-die law in, 119

Campbell, Joseph, 151

Cantwell, Maria, 181, 183

Cape Breton, Nova Scotia, 156

cemeteries as sculpture parks, 58

Chapel Hill, North Carolina, 28

childhood death, 159–166

    On Children and Death (Kübler-Ross),
      163

    Dianne Gray's experience, 162–166

    guilt, 168

    photographs of dead and dying
      children, 159–161

    withholding nutrition, 164–165

children. See talking to kids about death

Children's Hospital, Seattle, 77

Chur, Switzerland, 155

Cioffi, Sandy, 1, 4, 180–184

Coeio, 155

coffins, 153–154

compassionate inquiry, 96

conversations about death, 94–100

    Becky's experience, 94–98

    biases and heuristics, 98–100

    parable of two wolves, 100

    repressed memories, 96–97

Cook, Sheila, 141

cooking and eating as engine of culture,
    26–29

Coplan, Elizabeth, 30–31

Cora, 199–200

courtesy bias, 99

CPR, 65–66

cremation, 152–153

Cremation Solutions, 155

Cynthia, 3–4

Daly, Marcus, 153

David, 50–51

death

    festival on Vashon Island, 17–19

    at home, 48

    letting go, 54, 110, 190

    medical interventions, 63

    planning process, 12–13

    readiness to talk, 22–24

    shades of, 5

    See also discussions about death

death boutique, 57

Death Café, 28

death dinners

    at assisted-living facility, 25

    for college students, 77–78

    Cynthia's experience, 3–4

    with directors of End of Life
      Washington, 141

    email invitations, 23–24

    as gifts, 133

    for Hebb's family, 219–221

    for Maria's family, 40–44

    models for, 2–4, 29

    in Nashville, 25–26

    on 60 Minutes, 20

    "thirty days" prompt at, 39–40

    variety of answers to prompts, 41

Death Is Like a Light (Lundgren), 57, 104

Death Is Stupid (Higginbotham), 105

Death Over Dinner (DOD)

    doctors' reaction to, 38

    launch in Australia, 20

    success of, 19

Death Rounds, 70

death shaming, 208–209

Death with Dignity Law (2008), 119,
    121

deathbed feelings, 206–210
  death shaming, 208–209
  fear, 209
  Oliver Sacks's experience, 209–210
  Ruth's experience, 209
  sharpened focus, 209
The Denial of Death (Becker), 177
designing your own funeral or
    memorial, 55–61
  action-figure sculptures, 58
  The Greenwood Cemetery (Lundren), 57
  Holly's experience, 60–61
  Kiwi Coffin Club, 55–56
  names for stuffed animals, 60–61
  portraiture, 58
  suggestions for memorials, 61
  water ballet, 58–60
Devine, Megan, 169, 201
dialysis, 137
the Dinner Party, 189–190
Dinner with Your Muslim Neighbor
    (dinner series), 197–198
discussions about death
  abstract questions, 31
  books, 30
  with children, 25
  with college students, 77–78
  with dying people, 25
  effects of, 11–13
  email invitations, 23–24
  honesty and vulnerability, 33
  movies and theater, 30
  with people who have different
    views, 25–26
  reasons for, 24
  suggested approach, 29
doctor-assisted suicide, 117–123
  Brittany Maynard's experience,
    117–119*
  Death with Dignity Law (2008),
    119, 121

  euthanasia, 120
  Lester's experience, 141, 144–146
  patients' reactions to, 121–122
  right-to-die, 118–119
Doughty, Caitlyn, 30, 201
Drane, Alexandra "Alex," 45–48
Drury University, 77
Duncan, David Ewing, 39

Elisabeth Kübler-Ross Foundation, 162
Emily, 184–185
end-of-life care expenditures, 7
end-of-life experiences, 80–93
  Amanda Fisher's experience, 85–87
  being cared for, 81–82
  caring for dying person, 85–93
  dying person's acceptance, 80, 84
  Gail Ross's experience, 87–89
  Laurie Anderson's experience, 80
  Lisa's experience, 81–84
  Michael Hebb's experience, 89–93
  revelations, 90–91
  traditions, importance of, 83
End of Life Washington, 141–142
ending a conversation about death,
    216–218
Engage with Grace, 48
Epicurus, 221
euthanasia, 120

Farajallah, Hisham, 197
Farber, Stu, 71–72
fear of dying, 209
Feguer, Victor, 202
Fernandez, Carla, 188–190
Ferriss, Tim, 49
Fields, Torrie, 125
financial exploitation, 9
Finn, 219
Fisher, Amanda, 85–87
Fisher, M. F. K., 49

Flinn, Kathleen, 52–53
Flowers, Brian, 153
Flowers, Lennon, 188–190
food
    connection with love, 49
    as engine of culture, 28
    as part of mourning rituals, 195, 198
foods a departed loved one cooked for
        or with you, 49–54
    applesauce, 50
    chicken and dumplings, 53
    insomnia cure, 49
    Jenna's experience, 50
    Kathleen's experience, 53
    paella, 51
    Tim Ferriss's experience, 49
Forever Spot, 155
Frist, Bill, 26, 62
funerals, 55–61, 152, 156–158,
        211–215

Gawande, Atul, 7, 37
The Gift (Hyde), 133
Gill, Vince, 26
Give and Live, 137
Goldberg, Susan, 200
A Good Birth (Lyerly), 210
good death, 139–146
    Lester's experience, 141–146
    Tudy's experience, 139–140
Grant, Amy, 26
Grant, Angel, 20, 63, 94–95, 109–111
Gray, Austin, 162–165
Gray, Dianne, 162–166, 192
green burials, 153
Greenville, South Carolina, 63
The Greenwood Cemetery (Lundgren), 57
grieving, 188–201
    the Dinner Party, 189–190
    acceptance of loss, 4, 201
    anger, 201

Carla Fernandez's experience,
        188–190
Cora's experience, 199–200
    importance of traditions, 193–199
    Islamic rituals, 197–199
    Jewish rituals, 194–196
    Lennon Flowers's experience,
        188–190
    letting go, 110, 190
    loss of identity, 191–192
    nonjudgment, 193
    recovery from, 162
    repressing grief, 9–10
    waves of grief, 200–201
guilt, 65, 69, 165, 168, 178, 201
Guinea, 82
gyst.com (Get Your Shit Together), 76

Halifax, Roshi Joan, 69
Hamilton, Alexander, 28
Hargreaves, Henry, 202
Harman, Heather, 77–79
Harris, Richard, 15
Hazleton, Lesley, 173–175
hearts, primary functions of, 211
Hemingway, Ernest, 28
Higginbotham, Anastasia, 105–107
Hoffman, Allie, 13–14, 117–118
Holly, 60–61
home funeral, 156–157
homeostatic capacity, 171–172
hospice, 8, 54, 88–89, 94, 143, 165,
        206
"How Doctors Die" (Murray), 71
How to Get Your Shit Together (Reynolds),
        76
Huffington Post, 200
Hyde, Lewis, 133

India, death rituals in, 149–151
Infinity Burial Suit, 154–155

insomnia cure, 49
Into the Wild (Krakauer), 111
Islamic death rituals, 197–199

Jackson, Molly, 66–68
Jamaica, 81–84
Jefferson, Thomas, 28
Jenkinson, Stephen, 216
Jenna, 1, 4, 50, 101
Jeremy, 156–157
Jobs, Steve, 143
Joel, Billy, 125–126
Johnson, Lynette, 15, 159–161

Kahneman, Daniel, 98–99
Kalanithi, Elizabeth Acadia (Cady),
    186–187
Kalanithi, Lucy, 12
Kalanithi, Paul, 186–187
Karen, 101–102
Keely, Bevin, 58, 60
Kevorkian, Jack, 122
Keynes, John Maynard, 28
kidney donation, 137
Kiwi Coffin Club, 55–56
Koppel, Ted, 15
Krakauer, Jon, 111
Kreiling, Scott, 147–149
Kübler-Ross, Elisabeth, 12, 162–163,
    165, 206–208

LaCrosse, Wisconsin, 79
last meal, 202–205
    Anastasia Higginbotham's choice,
        203
    Bill Frist's choice, 204
    death-row last meals, 202
    Ira Byock's choice, 203
    Lucy Kalanithi's choice, 204
    Michael Hebb's choice, 204–205
    Tony Back's choice, 203

Last Week Tonight (TV show), 137
Lau-Lavie, Amichai, 196
Lee, Jae Rhim, 155
legacy, 179–187
    archeological collection, 184–185
    Bud's experience, 184–185
    children, 187
    honesty and tenacity, 184
    love of art, 180
    Paul Kalanithi's experience, 186–187
    Sandy Cioffi's experience, 180–184
    Tyler's experience, 179–180
Lester, 141–146
"Let It Be" (Beatles), 125
Letters to a Young Poet (Rilke), 109
Levine, Stephen, 159
life extension, 170–178
    answers at other death dinners,
        41–42
    bioresilience, 171–172
    death as a gift, 174
    evolutionary biology of loss, 171
    Joon Yun's interest in aging, 171–173
    Jo's experience, 42
    mission to continue our DNA,
        176–177
    views on life extension, 173–176,
        178
Lisa, 81–84
Lockwood, Maya, 114–116
Los Angeles Times, 120
Lunar Men, 28
Lundgren, Greg, 13, 56–58, 104, 162,
    179
Lundgren Monuments, 56–57
Lyerly, Anne Drapkin, 210

Madison, James, 28
Make-A-Wish Foundation, 51
Mary (Lester's sister), 142, 143, 145,
    146

Maté, Gabor, 96
Maxwell, Kathy, 139, 155, 213, 216–217
Maynard, Brittany, 14, 117–119
McCandless, Carine, 111–112
McLaughlin, Sally, 141–146
Meade, Michael, 12, 96
The Meadow (natural burial ground), 153
medical intervention, 62–72
    Angel Grant's experience, 63
    Bill Frist's experience, 62
    CPR, 65–66
    decision making, 67–69
    doctors' reactions to, 65–66, 71
    end-of-life care coursework, 67
    medical care costs, 68–69
    medicalization of death, 70, 158
    Molly Jackson's experience, 66–68
    Neil Orford's experience, 64–66
    nurses' roles, 62–63
    patient-doctor communication, 66–68
    Stu Farber's experience, 71–72
Medicare billing code for end-of-life conversations, 8
Megan, 112–113
Melbourne, Australia, 19
memory loss, 9
midlife sweet spot, 173
Miller, B.J., 208
Monica, 112–113
Mori, Kyoko, 116
Mt. Sinai School of Medicine, 7
Murray, Ken, 71

Nancy, 101
Nashville, Tennessee, 26
National Geographic magazine, 56
NBIA (neurodegenerative brain iron accumulation) disorder, 162

near-death experiences, 114–116
New York City, 87
New York Times, 39, 215
Nichols, Richard, 127
"No Seconds" photography series, 202
normalcy bias, 99

Obama, Barack, 137
Oliver, John, 137
On Children and Death (Kübler-Ross), 163
Oregon, right-to-die law in, 14
Orford, Neil, 64–66
organ donation, 131–138
    Bella's experience, 131–134
    The Gift (Hyde), 133
    Give and Live, 137
    organ donation summit, 137
    Organize, 136–137
    Pope Emeritus Benedict XVI, 135
    Rick Segal's experience, 134–136
    transplant issues, 132–133
    #WhenIDiePleaseTakeMyKidneys, 137
Organize, 136–137

palliative care, 47, 65, 67, 71, 120, 121, 207
Palliative Care Center of Excellence, 121
Palo Alto Longevity Prize, 171
Penn, Sean, 111
People magazine, 15, 118
People.com, 118
photographs of dead and dying children, 159–161
Picasso, Pablo, 28
Plato, 29
Pollan, Michael, 176
Polly's experience, 105–106
Porter, Catherine, 215

The Power of Myth (Campbell), 151
PTSD and suicide, 168

Questlove, 127

Ram Dass, 221
Recompose, 103, 152, 154
Reed, Lou, 80
regret, 10, 85, 87
revelations, 90–91
Reynolds, Chanel, 75–77, 192
right-to-die laws, 14, 119, 121
Rilke, Rainer Marie, 109
ritual and death, 151
Roberts, Seth, 49
Rolling Stone magazine, 80
The Roots, 127
Ross, Gail, 23, 87–89
Ross, Ken, 206–207
Ruwart, Mary, 122
Ruzek, Joe, 168

Saab, Amanda, 197
Sacks, Oliver, 209–210
Schwartz Rounds, 70
sculpture parks, 58
Seattle Times, 15, 59
Segal, Greg, 136–138
Segal, Rick, 134–136
senescence, 171
Serenbe, Georgia, 94
shame, 165
The Sharper the Knife, the Less You Cry
    (Flinn), 52
Shaw, Olivia, 39
Shields, John, 215
"Shots of Awe" (YouTube series), 174
Silva, Jason, 174–175
slow food movement, 157
Smoke Gets in Your Eyes (Doughty), 30
Socrates, 29

song at your funeral, 124–130
    Renee's experience, 130
    Richard Nichols's experience,
        127–129
    Torrie Fields's choice, 125–126
Soulumination, 15, 159
"Sound and Vision" (Bowie), 124
Spade, Katrina, 103–104, 152, 154
Stein, Gertrude, 28
Steve, 101
suicide, 10–11, 167–169
    See also doctor-assisted suicide
Suss, Ginny, 127, 129
Sutton, Willibel, 3–4
Sweet Crude (documentary film), 181

Tacoma News Tribune, 72
talking about you at your funeral,
        211–215
    Jessica's experience, 214, 215
    John Shield's experience, 215
    living funeral, 211–214
talking to kids about death, 101–107
    Angel's experience, 102–103
    Death Is Stupid (Higginbotham), 105
    environmental approach, 103–104
    Jenna's experience, 101
    Karen's experience, 101–102
    metaphysical approach, 104
    Nancy's experience, 101
    Polly's experience, 104–105
    relaxing into the uncertainty, 104
    Steve's experience, 101
Tea With Elisabeth (Fern Stewart Welch,
        editor), 166
Thiel, Peter, 175
Thinking, Fast and Slow (Kahneman),
        98–99
thirty days left to live
    Alex's experience, 45–48
    Maria's death dinner, 43–44

thirty days left to live (*continued*)
    not wanting to know, 45
    Olivia's answer, 39
    playing music, 44
    reading, 43
    reflecting on past, 44
    reluctance of doctors to tell patient,
        45
    sex, 42
    social worker's advice, 47
    time with family, 44
    traveling, 44
    Za's experience, 45–48
Time magazine, 165
transformation, 5
transplants, psychological issues with,
    132–133
Tudy, 139–140
Tuesdays with Morrie (Albom), 15
Tuxedo Park dinners, 28
Tversky, Amos, 98
Tyler, 74–75
Tyson, Neil deGrasse, 174

University of Washington School of
    Medicine, 66, 71
using this book, 31–33

Vashon Island, Washington, 17
"Vienna" (Joel), 125
Vital Talk, 67

Washington state, Death with Dignity
    law in, 121
Wells, Emily, 128–129
Wendy (Hebb's half-sister), 27
When Breath Becomes Air (Kalanithi), 12

Wiggins, Matt, 212
The Wild Truth (McCandless), 111
Williams, Kate, 56
Williams, Mary Elizabeth, 214–215
Williams, Sara, 28
wills, advance-care directives, and
    powers of attorney, 73–79
    Chanel Reynold's experience, 75–76
    college students' death discussions,
        77–78
    gyst.com, 76
    Heather Harman's experience,
        77–79
    How to Get Your Shit Together
        (Reynolds), 76
    Michael Hebb's experience, 73–74
    not wanting to be a burden, 78
    percent of US adults without a will,
        75
    relationship issues, 74–75
    Tyler's experience, 74–75
Witt, Ashleigh, 65
wolves, parable of, 100
women to apologize to, 91
Woolf, Virginia, 28
writing assignment, 91
Wu, Chyna, 5–6, 10
Wyatt, Karen, 10, 167–169

A Yarn and a Feed About Going Home,
    20–21
Yonder, Cassandra, 156–158
Yun, Joon, 170–173

Za's experience, 45–48
Zen Buddhism, 69–70
Zen Hospice Center, 208